lunches

Lunches

Second printing July 1998

Canadian Cataloguing in Publication Data

Main entry under title:
    Company's Coming for kids, lunches
Includes index.
ISBN 1-896891-36-5
    1. Luncheons—Juvenile literature. 2. Lunchbox cookery—Juvenile literature.

TX735.C64 1998   j641.5'3   C98-900348-5

Published simultaneously in Canada and the United States of America by
The Recipe Factory Inc.
in conjunction with
Company's Coming Publishing Limited
2311 - 96 Street
Edmonton, Alberta, Canada T6N 1G3
Tel: 403 • 450-6223   Fax: 403 • 450-1857

Company's Coming is a registered trademark owned by Company's Coming Publishing Limited

Company's Coming for Kids - Lunches

was created thanks to the dedicated efforts of the people and organizations listed below.

COMPANY'S COMING PUBLISHING LIMITED

Chairperson	Jean Paré
President	Grant Lovig
Vice President, Product Development	Kathy Knowles
Design Manager	Derrick Sorochan
Designers	Nora Cserny
	Jaclyn Draker
Typesetter	Marlene Crosbie
Project Assistant	Debbie Dixon

THE RECIPE FACTORY INC.

Research & Development Manager	Nora Prokop
Editor	Stephanie Amodio
Assistant Editor	Michelle White
Proofreader	Mimi Tindall
Test Kitchen Supervisor	Lynda Elsenheimer
Test Kitchen Staff	Ellen Bunjevac
	Allison Dosman
	Jacquie Elton
	Sharon Frietag
	Marg Steeden
	Audrey Thomas
	Pat Yukes
Photographer	Stephe Tate Photo
Food Stylist	Cora Lewyk
Prop Stylist	Gabriele McEleney

Our special thanks to the following businesses for providing extensive props for photography.

Creations by Design   *Mystique Pottery & Gifts*
Edmonton Wedding & Party Centre   *Stokes*
La Cache   *The Basket House*
Le Gnome   *The Bay*

Color separations, printing, and binding by
Friesens, Altona, Manitoba, Canada
Printed in Canada

Front Cover Photo:
1. Cinnamon Straws, page 22
2. Salmon Cups, page 42
3. Chocolate Chip Granola Bars, page 27
4. Hero Sandwich, page 102
5. Honey Mustard Dunk, page 28
6. Blueberry Pineapple Cooler, page 13
7. Peas 'N' Pasta Salad, page 97

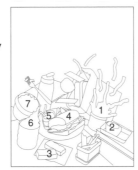

Back Cover Photo:
1. Hamburger Soup, page 124
2. Spicy Chicken Fingers, page 41
3. Marinated Vegetables, page 91
4. Chocolate Bar Cookies, page 21
5. Apple-Crisp Cookies, page 15

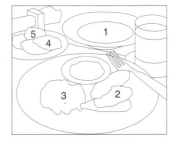

table of contents

Company's Coming cookbooks

COMPANY'S COMING SERIES

150 Delicious Squares	Lunches
Casseroles	Pies
Muffins & More	Light Recipes
Salads	Microwave Cooking
Appetizers	Preserves
Desserts	Light Casseroles
Soups & Sandwiches	Chicken, Etc.
Holiday Entertaining	Kids Cooking
Cookies	Fish & Seafood
Vegetables	Breads
Main Courses	Meatless Cooking
Pasta	Cooking for Two
Cakes	Breakfasts & Brunches
Barbecues	Slow Cooker Recipes
Dinners of the World	September 1998 - NEW

SELECT SERIES

Sauces & Marinades	30-Minute Meals
Ground Beef	Make-Ahead Salads
Beans & Rice	No-Bake Desserts

INDIVIDUAL TITLES

Company's Coming for Christmas
Beef Today!
The Family Table
Kids Only - Snacks
Low-Fat Cooking
Company's Coming for Kids - Lunches

foreword

ime for lunch? How about a crispy cold salad or a piping hot pizza. Have to pack a school lunch? Pick from an assortment of veggie dips or choose a trendy wrap sandwich. For more help, check the menu suggestions on pages 10 and 11.

Be sure to refer to the **Get Ready! Get Set!** list before you start a recipe. Every utensil or piece of equipment you will need is listed in the order you will use it!

You'll see that some recipes have a special icon beside their name—here's what they mean:

 You'll have to chill this recipe in the refrigerator before serving.

 This recipe has to be baked in the oven. (Don't forget the oven mitts!)

Now that you have your book in hand, and are all set to begin, remember one important last step—whether you eat in or take out, always clean up when you're done. Your parents will appreciate it, and so will your school!

watch out! safety in the kitchen tips

1 Never touch anything electrical with wet hands.

2 Always pull out a plug by holding and pulling on the plug itself, not the cord.

3 Keep saucepan handles turned inward on top of the stove.

4 Know how to properly use all appliances before starting.

5 Use well-insulated oven mitts to handle hot dishes.

6 Turn off burners and oven, and unplug small appliances when not in use.

A note to parents

This book is intended for your children to use. It has been especially written for kids aged 8 to 15 years. Please supervise them when necessary. The handling of sharp knives, boiling liquids, and hot pans needs to be monitored carefully with younger children.

glossary

Bake   To cook in an oven preheated to the temperature it says in the recipe. Use either the bottom rack or center rack.

Batter   A mixture of flour, liquid and other ingredients that can be thin (such as pancake batter) or thick (such as muffin batter).

Beat   To mix two or more ingredients with a spoon, fork or electric mixer, using a circular motion.

Blend   To mix two or more ingredients together with a spoon, fork, electric mixer, or electric blender until combined.

Boil   To heat a liquid in a saucepan until bubbles rise in a steady pattern and break on the surface. Steam also starts to rise from the surface.

Broil   To cook under the top heating element in the oven. Use either the top rack or the upper rack.

Break An Egg   Tap the side of an egg on the edge of a bowl or cup to crack the shell. Place the tips of both thumbs in the crack and open the shell, letting the egg yolk and egg white drop into the bowl.

Chill   To refrigerate until cold.

Chop   To cut food carefully into small pieces with a sharp knife on a cutting board; to chop finely is to cut foods as small as you can.

Combine   To put two or more ingredients together.

Cream   To beat an ingredient or combination of ingredients until the mixture is soft, smooth, and "creamy."

Cut In   To combine solid fat (such as butter or margarine) with dry ingredients (such as flour) using a fork or pastry blender until the mixture looks like big crumbs the size of green peas.

Dice   To cut food into small ¼ inch (6 mm) cube-shaped pieces.

Dip (into)   To lower into a liquid either part way or all the way.

Drain   To strain away an unwanted liquid (such as water, fruit juice, or grease) using a colander or strainer. Drain water or juice over the kitchen sink or in a bowl. Drain grease into a metal can, refrigerate, then throw away in the garbage after it hardens.

Drizzle   To dribble drops or lines of glaze or icing over food in a random manner from tines of a fork or the end of a spoon.

Fold   To mix gently, using a rubber spatula, by cutting down in the center and lifting towards the edge of the bowl. Use a "down, up, over" movement, turning the bowl as you repeat.

Garnish   To decorate food with edible condiments such as parsley sprigs, fruit slices or vegetable cut-outs.

Heat   To make something warm or hot by placing the saucepan on the stove burner that is turned on to the level it says in the recipe.

Knead   To work dough into a smooth putty-like mass by pressing and folding using the heels of your hands.

Let Stand   To let a baked product cool slightly on a wire rack or hot pad, while still in its baking pan.

Mash   To squash cooked or very ripe foods with a fork or potato masher.

Melt   To heat a solid food such as butter, margarine, cheese or chocolate, until it turns into a liquid. Be careful not to burn it.

Mix (see **Combine**)

Mixing Just Until Moistened   To stir dry ingredients with liquid ingredients until dry ingredients are just wet. Mixture will still be lumpy.

Process   To mix or cut up food in a blender (or food processor) until it is the way it says in the recipe.

Sauté   To cook food quickly in a small amount of oil in a frying pan, wok, or special sauté pan over medium heat.

Scramble-Fry   To brown ground meat in hot oil using a spoon, fork or pancake lifter to break up the meat into small crumb-like pieces as it cooks.

Scrape   To use a rubber spatula to remove as much of a mixture as possible from inside a bowl or saucepan.

Separate An Egg (see **Break An Egg**)   Once the shell is open, carefully keep the egg yolk in one half shell and let the egg white drip into a small bowl or cup. Carefully pour the yolk into the other half shell, again letting any egg white drip into the bowl or cup. Be careful that the yolk does not break. Continue until there is no more egg white, except in the bowl or cup.

Simmer   To cook liquids in a saucepan over a low heat on the stove burner so that slow bubbles appear on the surface around the sides of the liquid.

Slice   To cut foods such as apples, carrots, tomatoes, meat or bread into thin sections or pieces, using a sharp knife.

Spoon (into)   To move ingredients from one container to another, using a spoon to scoop from one and drop into the other.

Spread   To cover the surface of one product (generally a more solid food) with another product (generally a softer food such as icing or butter).

Stir   To mix two or more ingredients with a spoon, using a circular motion.

Toast   To brown lightly in a toaster or frying pan or under the broiler in the oven.

Toss   To mix salad ingredients lightly with a lifting motion, using two forks, two spoons or salad tongs.

equipment & utensils

Baking sheet

Bread knife

Broiler pan

Casserole dish

Colander

Blender

Cookie sheet

Cutting board

Dry measures

Electric frying pan

Electric mixer

Frying pan

Hot pad

Ice-cream scoop

Loaf pan

Grater

Liquid measures

Measuring spoons

Mixing spoons (long-handled)

Microwave oven

Mixing bowls

Muffin pan

Oblong baking dish

Oblong baking pan

Oven mitts

Pancake lifter

Paper muffin cup

Pastry brush

Pastry blender

Pie plate

Pizza cutter

Pizza pan

Potato Masher

Rolling pin

Round cake pan

Rubber spatula

Saucepan

Sharp knife

Sieve or strainer

Square baking pan

Table knife, fork & spoon

Burners

Top Rack

Center Rack

Upper Rack

Bottom Rack

Toaster

Tongs

Oven with rack positions

Whisk

Wire rack

home lunch menu suggestions

Home Lunch #1
Chicken Thumbs, page 38
Dilly Pickle Dip, page 28
Potato Salad, page 88
Easy Raisin Cookies, page 23
Melon Milk Shake, page 12

Home Lunch #2
Loaded Quesadilla, page 73
Peas 'N' Pasta Salad, page 97
Applesauce Jellied Dessert, page 23
Strawberry Banana Slushy, page 12

Home Lunch #3
Nacho Skins, page 39
Corn Chowder, page 128
Hot Tortilla Dip, page 32 (with vegetables and
    tortilla chips)

Home Lunch #4
Pita Pizzas, page 81
Color-Full Bean Soup, page 130
Sour Cream & Onion Dip, page 30
    (with vegetables)
Lemon Cola Float, page 13

Home Lunch #5
Creamy Beef 'N' Pasta, page 57
Cottage Cheese Salad, page 95
Apricot Logs, page 16
Eggnog, page 14

Home Lunch #6
Creamy Macaroni & Cheese, page 60
Tomato & Mozza Salad, page 93
S'Mores Squares, page 19
Strawberry Pineapple Cooler, page 13

Home Lunch #7
Quick Bread "Sandwich", page 55
Hamburger Soup, page 124
Garlic Cheese Dressing, page 29
    (with vegetables)
Snap Gingers, page 25

Home Lunch #8
Mexican Stir-Fry Sandwich, page 131
Vegetable Chowder, page 127
Banana Raisin Bars, page 24

bag lunch menu suggestions

Bag Lunch #1
Salmon Cups, page 42
Seeded Cheese, page 40
Rice Salad, page 92
Apple-Crisp Cookies, page 15

Bag Lunch #2
Veggie Bagel, page 100
Cucumber & Pea Salad, page 92
Chocolate Chip Granola Bars, page 27
Raspberry Pineapple Cooler, page 13

Bag Lunch #3
Individual Stuffed Pizzas, page 82
Marinated Vegetables, page 91
Cinnamon Straws, page 22
Blueberry Pineapple Cooler, page 13

Bag Lunch #4
Hero Sandwich, page 102
Tortellini Salad, page 87
Garlic Mustard Dip, page 29 (with vegetables)
Chocolate Bar Cookies, page 21

Bag Lunch #5
Barbecue Beef Buns, page 111
Bean & Tomato Salad, page 94
Bolts 'N' Things, page 120

Bag Lunch #6
Ham & Cheese Delights, page 133
Peanut Butter Pudding Dip, page 31
   (with fresh fruit)
Fruity Granola, page 118
Veggie Cooler, page 14

Bag Lunch #7
Vegetable Roll, page 135
Ham & Melon Kabobs, page 40
Pepper-Corn Crackers, page 44
Spicy Corn Corn, page 122

Bag Lunch #8
Roast Beef Rolls, page 132
Broccoli 'N' Rice, page 63
Gingerbran Cream Muffins, page 26

Melon Milk Shake

Very refreshing.

1.	Cantaloupe (or honeydew melon), see Note	½	½
2.	Milk	1½ cups	375 mL
	Liquid honey	1 tbsp.	15 mL

- table spoon
- small bowl
- liquid measures
- measuring spoons
- blender

1. Remove the seeds of the melon with the spoon. Scoop the melon out of the skin into the bowl. Freeze for 1 hour until solid. Cover with plastic wrap if freezing longer.

2. Put the milk and honey into the blender. Add the frozen melon. Process until smooth. Drink immediately. Makes about 4 cups (1 L).

Note: The amount of the drink will depend on the size of the cantaloupe or melon.

Strawberry Banana Slushy

A thick, rich shake.

1.	Lemon, vanilla or strawberry yogurt	¾ cup	175 mL
	Skim milk powder	2 tbsp.	30 mL
	Banana	1	1
	Milk	1 cup	250 mL
2.	Large frozen strawberries	5	5

- dry measures
- measuring spoons
- liquid measures
- blender

1. Put the yogurt, milk powder, banana and milk into the blender. Process until smooth.

2. While the blender is processing, add the strawberries, 1 at a time, through the opening in the lid. Process until smooth and creamy. Makes 3½ cups (875 mL).

Strawberry Pineapple Cooler

A lovely pink color with light pink foam on top. The soft drink adds a little fizz.

1.	Pineapple juice, chilled	1 cup	250 mL
	Skim milk powder	2 tbsp.	30 mL
	Large frozen strawberries	3	3
2.	Ginger ale (or club soda), optional	½ cup	125 mL

- liquid measures
- measuring spoons
- blender
- mixing spoon

1. Combine the pineapple juice and milk powder in the blender. Cover and process for 10 seconds. While the blender is processing, add the strawberries, 1 at a time, through the opening in the lid. Process until smooth.

2. Stir in the ginger ale if you wish to have a fizzy cooler. Makes 1⅓ cups (325 mL).

RASPBERRY PINEAPPLE COOLER: Follow the directions for the Strawberry Pineapple Cooler, substituting ½ cup (125 mL) of raspberries for the strawberries.

BLUEBERRY PINEAPPLE COOLER: Follow the directions for the Strawberry Pineapple Cooler, substituting ½ cup (125 mL) of blueberries for the strawberries.

Pictured on the front cover.

Lemon Cola Float

The perfect beverage to have at home as a treat for lunch.

1.	Cola soft drink, chilled	1 cup	250 mL
	Scoops of lemon sherbet	2	2

- liquid measures
- tall glass
- ice-cream scoop

1. Pour the soft drink into the glass. Add the lemon sherbet. Makes 1 float.

Pictured on page 53.

Veggie Cooler

A delicious way to get your vegetables. Smooth and refreshing.

- liquid measures
- dry measures
- blender

1.	Tomato juice	1½ cups	375 mL
	Chopped celery	½ cup	125 mL
	Chopped cucumber	½ cup	125 mL
	Grated carrot	½ cup	125 mL
	Hot pepper sauce, dash (optional)		

1. Put all 5 ingredients into the blender. Process until smooth. Cover. Chill in the refrigerator for several hours or overnight. Makes 2⅓ cups (575 mL).

Pictured on page 90.

Eggnog

A perfect homemade version for the younger set.

- measuring spoons
- blender
- liquid measures
- ice-cream scoop

1.	Large egg (see Note)	1	1
	Granulated sugar	1 tbsp.	15 mL
2.	Vanilla flavoring	½ tsp.	2 mL
	Salt, sprinkle		
	Milk	½ cup	125 mL
	Ground nutmeg	⅛ tsp.	0.5 mL
3.	Scoops of vanilla ice cream	2	2

1. Put the egg and sugar into the blender. Process until thick and lemon colored.

2. Add the next 4 ingredients. Process.

3. Add the ice cream. Process until smooth. Serve immediately. Makes 1 cup (250 mL).

Note: Keep the egg in the refrigerator until you are ready to use it.

Pictured on page 107.

Apple-Crisp Cookies

A nice drop cookie that keeps its shape when it bakes. Moist, with a crunch.

1.			
Tub margarine		²⁄₃ cup	150 mL
Brown sugar, packed		1 cup	250 mL
Large eggs, fork-beaten		2	2
Vanilla flavoring		1 tsp.	5 mL
Quick-cooking rolled oats (not instant)		1½ cups	375 mL
2.			
All-purpose flour		1½ cups	375 mL
Baking powder		1 tsp.	5 mL
Ground cinnamon		½ tsp.	2 mL
Salt		½ tsp.	2 mL
Medium apples, peeled, cored and finely chopped		2	2
Chopped pecans (or walnuts), optional		½ cup	125 mL

- cookie sheet
- dry measures
- medium bowl
- electric mixer
- measuring spoons
- mixing spoon
- small bowl
- oven mitts
- wire rack
- pancake lifter
- waxed paper

1. Place the oven rack in the center position. Turn the oven on to 350°F (175°C). Grease the cookie sheet. Beat the margarine and sugar together on low speed in the medium bowl. Add the eggs and vanilla. Beat together well on high speed. Add the rolled oats. Stir.

2. Combine the flour, baking powder, cinnamon and salt in the small bowl. Add to the margarine mixture. Stir. Add the apple and pecans and mix well. Drop by level tablespoonfuls onto the cookie sheet. Bake in the oven for 15 minutes. Use the oven mitts to remove the cookie sheet to the wire rack. Let stand for 2 minutes. Use the pancake lifter to remove the cookies to the waxed paper on the counter. Cool completely. Makes 24 cookies.

Pictured on the back cover.

Apricot Logs chill

Pure and natural. All fruit and coconut.

- dry measures
- measuring spoons
- medium microwave-safe casserole dish
- microwave oven
- blender
- mixing spoon
- medium bowl
- waxed paper
- plastic wrap
- sharp knife

1.	Dried apricots (about 40) Water Juice of 1 orange	1½ cups 1 tbsp.	375 mL 15 mL
2.	Grated peel of 1 orange Flake coconut	½ cup	125 mL
3.	Flake coconut	⅔ cup	150 mL

1. Put the apricots and water into the casserole dish. Cover. Microwave on high (100%) for 2 minutes until moist and plump. Put the apricot mixture and orange juice into the blender. Process, stopping the blender and stirring every few seconds, until the apricots are very finely chopped. Put the mixture into the bowl.

2. Mix in the orange peel and the first amount of coconut. Divide the mixture in half. Roll into two 6 inch (15 cm) logs.

3. Place the second amount of coconut on the waxed paper. Roll the logs in the coconut until well coated. Cover each log with plastic wrap. Place in the refrigerator to chill. Cut into 1 inch (2.5 cm) pieces. Makes 2 logs.

Pictured on page 17.

Variation: Roll the mixture into small balls rather than into logs, then roll in the coconut and chill. Makes about 18 one inch (2.5 cm) balls.

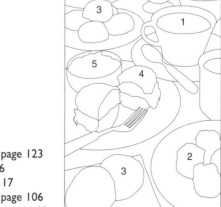

1. Easy Macaroni Soup, page 123
2. Apricot Logs, page 16
3. Egg Roll Buns, page 117
4. Pepper Cheese Roll, page 106
5. Cottage Cheese Salad, page 95

S'Mores Squares

Wow! A whole pan of s'mores! Be sure to use a hot, wet knife for cutting. These seem hard but are really just chewy.

1.	Whole graham crackers	48	48
2.	Tub margarine	2 tbsp.	30 mL
	Corn syrup	½ cup	125 mL
	Milk (or semisweet) chocolate chips	1½ cups	375 mL
3.	Miniature marshmallows	2 cups	500 mL

- 9 x 9 inch (22 x 22 cm) square baking pan
- plastic bag
- rolling pin
- measuring spoons
- dry measures
- large microwave-safe bowl
- waxed paper
- microwave oven
- mixing spoon
- sharp knife

1. Grease the baking pan. Put the graham crackers into the plastic bag. Coarsely crush the graham crackers with the rolling pin.

2. Place the margarine, corn syrup and chocolate chips in the bowl. Cover with waxed paper. Microwave on high (100%) for 2 minutes. Stir well. Microwave on high (100%) for 1 minute until the mixture is boiling.

3. Mix in the crushed graham crackers. Stir in the marshmallows. Press in the baking pan. Let stand at room temperature. Mixture will become quite hard and chewy. Carefully cut with the knife, dipping it in hot water after each cut. Cuts into 26 squares.

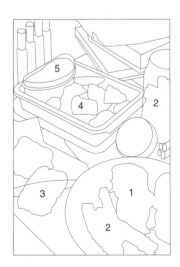

1. Vegetable Roll, page 135
2. Seeded Cheese, page 40
3. Banana Raisin Bars, page 24
4. Crispy Chicken Cracky, page 43
5. Garlic Mustard Dip, page 29

Applesauce

Great by itself, or use in other recipes.

- cutting board
- sharp knife
- medium microwave-safe bowl
- measuring spoons
- plastic wrap
- microwave oven
- oven mitts
- hot pad
- mixing spoon
- potato masher (or table fork)

1.			
Large apples, peeled		3	3
Brown sugar, packed		1 tbsp.	15 mL
Ground cinnamon, sprinkle			

1. Using the cutting board, slice the apple off of the core in fairly large pieces, approximately 8. Discard the core. Put the slices into the bowl. Sprinkle with the sugar and cinnamon. Cover the bowl with plastic wrap. Microwave on high (100%) for 5 minutes. Using the oven mitts, remove the bowl from the oven to the hot pad. Slowly fold back the plastic wrap, being very careful not to burn yourself as the hot steam escapes. Stir. Cover the bowl again and microwave on high (100%) for 5 minutes. Using the oven mitts, remove the bowl to the hot pad. Let the mixture stand for 15 minutes to cool. Mash the cooled mixture with the potato masher until it is a chunky consistency. Makes 1⅔ cups (400 mL).

Yummy Oatmeal Bars

Sweet and crunchy. Cuts well. Dough is very stiff but everything will mix in eventually.

- 9 x 9 inch (22 x 22 cm) square baking pan
- liquid measures
- dry measures
- large microwave-safe bowl
- mixing spoon
- microwave oven

1.			
Liquid honey		⅔ cup	150 mL
Peanut butter		½ cup	125 mL
Butterscotch chips		¾ cup	175 mL
Large marshmallows		10	10
2. Quick-cooking rolled oats (not instant)		2 cups	500 mL
Sunflower seeds		¼ cup	60 mL
Crisp rice cereal		1 cup	250 mL
Raisins (or chopped dates)		1 cup	250 mL

Continued on the next page.

1. Grease the pan. Stir the honey and peanut butter together in the bowl. Microwave, uncovered, on high (100%) for 2 minutes until hot and bubbly. Stir in the butterscotch chips and marshmallows until melted. Microwave on medium (50%) for 30 seconds, if needed, to finish melting the marshmallows.

2. Stir in the remaining 4 ingredients. Press well in the pan. Cool. Cuts into 27 bars.

Chocolate Bar Cookies

Dotted with chocolate. Soft and chewy.

1.	Hard margarine, softened	½ cup	125 mL
	Brown sugar, packed	⅓ cup	75 mL
	Granulated sugar	⅓ cup	75 mL
2.	Vanilla flavoring	1 tsp.	5 mL
	Large egg, fork-beaten	1	1
3.	All-purpose flour	1¼ cups	300 mL
	Baking soda	½ tsp.	2 mL
	Salt	¼ tsp.	1 mL
4.	Butter crunch chocolate bars	2 × 1½ oz.	2 × 39 g

1. Place the oven rack in the center position. Turn the oven on to 375°F (190°C). Cream the margarine and both sugars together in the bowl until smooth.

2. Stir in the vanilla flavoring and egg.

3. Add the flour, baking soda and salt. Mix well, scraping down the sides of the bowl.

4. Place the chocolate bars in the plastic bag. Break the bars into chunky pieces by hitting them with the rolling pin. Stir the chunks into the dough. Drop by teaspoonfuls, about 2 inches (5 cm) apart, onto the ungreased cookie sheet. Bake in the oven for 10 minutes until the edges are browned. Centers will stay soft. Use the oven mitts to remove the cookie sheet to the wire rack. Let stand for 1 minute. Remove the cookies to the waxed paper to cool completely. Makes 28 cookies.

Pictured on the back cover.

GET READY GET SET!

- dry measures
- medium bowl
- measuring spoons
- mixing spoons
- thick plastic bag
- rolling pin
- cookie sheet
- oven mitts
- wire rack
- waxed paper

Cinnamon Straws hot

Try these dipped in applesauce. These freeze well.

1.	Envelope pie crust mix	1 × 9½ oz.	1 × 270 g
	Cold water	6 tbsp.	100 mL
2.	Tub margarine, divided	2 tbsp.	30 mL
	Brown sugar, packed	2 tbsp.	30 mL
	Ground cinnamon	1 tbsp.	15 mL
	All-purpose flour, as needed, to prevent sticking while rolling		

1. Place the oven rack in the center position. Turn the oven on to 400°F (205°C). Place the pie crust mix in the bowl. Add the cold water, 1 tbsp. (15 mL) at a time, stirring with the fork after each addition. Form the dough into a ball. Divide the dough in half. Sprinkle some flour on the working surface. Roll out ½ of the dough into a 5 × 11 inch (12.5 × 28 cm) rectangle, about ⅛ inch (3 mm) thick.

2. Spread 1 tbsp. (15 mL) of the margarine over ½ of the rectangle, right to the edges. Combine the sugar and cinnamon in the small cup. Sprinkle ½ of the sugar mixture over the margarine. Fold the uncovered pastry half over the cinnamon half. Gently roll into a 5 × 11 inch (12.5 × 28 cm) rectangle, ⅛ inch (3 mm) thick. Set on the cutting board. Use the sharp knife to cut strips across the dough, each strip about ½ inch (12 mm) wide. Twist each strip 2 to 3 times and lay them on the ungreased baking sheet. Repeat with the second ½ of the dough. Bake in the oven for about 11 minutes until crisp and lightly browned. Use the oven mitts to remove the baking sheet to the wire rack. Makes 44 to 48 straws.

Pictured on the front cover.

- medium bowl
- measuring spoons
- table fork
- rolling pin
- ruler
- table knife
- small cup
- mixing spoon
- cutting board
- sharp knife
- baking sheet
- oven mitts
- wire rack

Applesauce Jellied Dessert chill

You may want to put this dessert into four small plastic containers with lids. Then you can take it to school in your lunch bag; it will remain solid for several hours at room temperature after chilling.

1.	Package strawberry, cherry or lime-flavored gelatin (jelly powder)	1 x 3 oz.	1 x 85 g
	Boiling water	¾ cup	175 mL
	Applesauce, page 20, (or 1 can 14 oz., 398 mL)	1⅔ cups	400 mL

- liquid measures
- medium bowl
- dry measures
- mixing spoon
- 4 small dessert bowls

1. Dissolve the gelatin in the boiling water in the bowl. Stir in the applesauce. Divide the mixture among the bowls. Chill in the refrigerator for about 3 hours. Serves 4.

Easy Raisin Cookies hot

This is a very easy cookie to make using a cake mix.

1.	Yellow cake mix, 2 layer size	1	1
	Large eggs, fork-beaten	2	2
	Cooking oil	⅓ cup	75 mL
	Water	2 tbsp.	30 mL
	Raisins	1 cup	250 mL

- cookie sheet
- liquid measures
- measuring spoons
- dry measures
- large bowl
- mixing spoon
- oven mitts
- wire rack
- pancake lifter
- waxed paper

1. Place the oven rack in the center position. Turn the oven on to 350°F (175°C). Grease the cookie sheet. Combine all 5 ingredients in the bowl. Stir until the cake mix is moistened and smooth. (Small lumps are fine.) Drop by tablespoonfuls onto the cookie sheet. Bake in the oven for 18 minutes until golden. Use the oven mitts to remove the cookie sheet to the wire rack. Let stand for 2 minutes. Use the pancake lifter to remove the cookies to the waxed paper on the counter. Cool completely. Makes 33 cookies.

Pictured on page 90.

Banana Raisin Bars hot

Soft and chewy. These will remind you of banana bread.

- 9 x 13 inch
  (22 x 33 cm)
  oblong baking pan
- dry measures
- large bowl
- measuring spoons
- small bowl
- electric mixer
- mixing spoon
- oven mitts
- wire rack

1.			
	Quick-cooking rolled oats (not instant)	3 cups	750 mL
	Long thread coconut	1 cup	250 mL
	Raisins	1 cup	250 mL
	Sunflower seeds	½ cup	125 mL
	Peanuts, chopped	½ cup	125 mL
2.	Tub margarine	½ cup	125 mL
	Corn syrup	3 tbsp.	50 mL
	Liquid honey	3 tbsp.	50 mL
	Large egg	1	1
	Vanilla flavoring	1 tsp.	5 mL
	Mashed banana	⅓ cup	75 mL

1. Place the oven rack in the center position. Turn the oven on to 325°F (160°C). Grease the baking pan. Combine the first 5 ingredients in the large bowl.

2. Beat the next 6 ingredients together with the electric mixer on high speed in the small bowl until light and fluffy. Stir into the rolled oat mixture and combine well. Spread in the baking pan and press down well. Bake in the oven for 50 minutes until firm and golden. Use the oven mitts to remove the baking pan to the wire rack. Cool. Cuts into 20 bars.

Pictured on page 18.

Variation: Substitute ½ cup (125 mL) of applesauce for the banana and add ⅛ tsp. (0.5 mL) of ground cinnamon.

Snap Gingers hot

Round and flat with a chewy texture. Ginger flavor through and through.

1.	**Hard margarine, softened**	**½ cup**	**125 mL**
	Granulated sugar	**⅔ cup**	**150 mL**
2.	**Molasses (not blackstrap)**	**¼ cup**	**60 mL**
	Large egg, fork-beaten	**1**	**1**
3.	**All-purpose flour**	**1½ cups**	**375 mL**
	Baking soda	**1½ tsp.**	**7 mL**
	Ground ginger	**1½ tsp.**	**7 mL**
	Salt	**¼ tsp.**	**1 mL**
4.	**Granulated sugar, for coating**		

- dry measures
- small bowl
- liquid measures
- mixing spoon
- rubber spatula
- measuring spoons
- cookie sheet
- drinking glass
- oven mitts
- wire rack
- waxed paper

1. Place the oven rack in the center position. Turn the oven on to 375°F (190°C). Cream the margarine and first amount of sugar together well in the bowl.

2. Stir in the molasses and egg until well mixed, occasionally scraping down the sides of the bowl with the rubber spatula.

3. Stir in the next 4 ingredients until well blended.

4. Make 1 inch (2.5 cm) balls with the dough. Roll each ball in the second amount of sugar to coat. Place on the ungreased cookie sheet, 2 inches (5 cm) apart. Flatten each ball with the bottom of the glass. Bake in the oven for 7 minutes. Use the oven mitts to remove the cookie sheet to the wire rack. Let stand for 1 minute. Remove the cookies to the waxed paper to cool completely. Makes 26 cookies.

Pictured on page 36.

Gingerbran Cream Muffins (hot)

Cream cheese filling is the perfect touch.

- 12 large muffin papers
- muffin pan (for 12 muffins)
- measuring spoons
- small bowl
- mixing spoon
- liquid measures
- dry measures
- medium bowl
- large bowl
- wooden toothpick
- oven mitts
- wire rack

1.	Cream cheese, softened	4 oz.	125 g
	Granulated sugar	2 tbsp.	30 mL
	Finely grated orange peel	1 tsp.	5 mL
2.	Large eggs, fork-beaten	2	2
	Cooking oil	¼ cup	60 mL
	Buttermilk (or reconstituted from powder)	½ cup	125 mL
	Molasses (not blackstrap)	⅓ cup	75 mL
	Natural bran	½ cup	125 mL
3.	All-purpose flour	1¾ cups	425 mL
	Brown sugar, packed	½ cup	125 mL
	Baking soda	1 tsp.	5 mL
	Baking powder	½ tsp.	2 mL
	Ground ginger	2 tsp.	10 mL
	Ground allspice	½ tsp.	2 mL

1. Place the oven rack in the center position. Turn the oven on to 350°F (175°C). Place the muffin papers in the pan. Combine the cream cheese, sugar and orange peel in the small bowl. Mix until smooth. Set aside.

2. Combine the next 5 ingredients in the medium bowl. Stir. Let stand for 5 minutes.

3. Combine the next 6 ingredients in the large bowl. Mix well. Make a well in the center. Pour the milk mixture into the well. Stir just to moisten. Do not stir too much. Divide the batter among the 12 muffin cups. Gently spoon a rounded teaspoon of the cream cheese mixture into the center of each muffin. Bake in the oven for 25 minutes until golden. The toothpick inserted in the center of 2 or 3 muffins should come out clean. Use the oven mitts to remove the muffin pan to the wire rack. Let stand for 10 minutes. Remove the muffins from the pan to the rack to cool. Makes 12 muffins.

Pictured on page 72.

Chocolate Chip Granola Bars 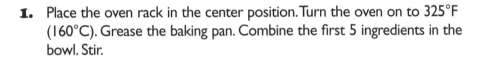 (hot)

Chewy with chocolate and coconut. Holds together well.

1.			
Graham cracker crumbs	1 cup	250 mL
Flake coconut	1 cup	250 mL
Granola	1½ cups	375 mL
Semisweet chocolate chips	1 cup	250 mL
Chopped pecans (or other nuts), optional	¼ cup	60 mL

2.			
Sweetened condensed milk	11 oz.	300 mL
Hard margarine, melted	⅓ cup	75 mL

- 9 × 13 inch (22 × 33 cm) oblong baking pan
- dry measures
- medium bowl
- mixing spoon
- oven mitts
- wire rack

1. Place the oven rack in the center position. Turn the oven on to 325°F (160°C). Grease the baking pan. Combine the first 5 ingredients in the bowl. Stir.

2. Drizzle the condensed milk and margarine over the mixture. Mix well. Press well in the baking pan. Bake in the oven for 30 minutes until lightly golden. Use the oven mitts to remove the baking pan to the wire rack. Cool. Cuts into 20 bars.

Pictured on the front cover.

 **Did you know?**

When baking muffins (or other food) in a muffin pan, if you don't use all the cups, fill the empty muffin cups half-way with water. This will prevent the muffin pan from burning.

Honey Mustard Dunk

Great served with ham, sausages or veggies.

1.	Mayonnaise (or salad dressing)	½ cup	125 mL
	Liquid honey	2 tbsp.	30 mL
	Prepared mustard	2 tsp.	10 mL

- dry measures
- measuring spoons
- small bowl
- mixing spoon

1. Put all 3 ingredients into the bowl. Mix until smooth. Makes ⅔ cup (150 mL).

Pictured on the front cover.

Dilly Pickle Dip chill

A great dip for vegetables or Chicken Thumbs, page 38, or Spicy Chicken Fingers, page 41.

1.	Sour cream	½ cup	125 mL
	Plain yogurt	½ cup	125 mL
	Finely chopped dill pickles, blotted dry with paper towel	⅓ cup	75 mL
	Dill weed	1 tsp.	5 mL
	Salt	¼ tsp.	1 mL
	Pepper, sprinkle		

- dry measures
- small bowl
- mixing spoon
- measuring spoons
- plastic wrap

1. Combine the sour cream and yogurt in the bowl. Stir together well. Add the remaining 4 ingredients. Stir. Cover with plastic wrap. Chill in the refrigerator for 1 hour to blend the flavors. Makes 1¼ cups (300 mL).

Dips & Spreads

Garlic Cheese Dressing chill

Take to school to dip fresh veggies in.

- dry measures
- measuring spoons
- small bowl
- mixing spoon

1.
Mayonnaise (or salad dressing)	½ cup	125 mL
Lemon juice	1 tbsp.	15 mL
Garlic powder	¼ tsp.	1 mL
Onion powder	⅛ tsp.	0.5 mL
Water	1 tbsp.	15 mL
Grated mozzarella cheese	¼ cup	60 mL
Simulated bacon bits (or 1 bacon slice, cooked and crumbled)	1 tbsp.	15 mL

1. Combine all 7 ingredients in the bowl. Mix well. Chill in the refrigerator for 15 minutes to blend the flavors. Makes ¾ cup (175 mL).

Garlic Mustard Dip chill

Put in a small container to take for lunch. Great for veggies.

- dry measures
- measuring spoons
- small bowl
- mixing spoon
- plastic wrap

1.
Mayonnaise (or salad dressing)	⅓ cup	75 mL
Sour cream	⅔ cup	150 mL
Prepared mustard	1 tbsp.	15 mL
Garlic powder	⅛ tsp.	0.5 mL
Salt, sprinkle		
Pepper, sprinkle		

1. Combine all 6 ingredients in the bowl. Mix well. Cover with plastic wrap. Chill in the refrigerator for 30 minutes to blend the flavors. Store any remaining dip in the refrigerator for up to 3 days. Makes 1¼ cups (300 mL).

Pictured on page 18.

Creamy Garlic Dip  chill

If you like Caesar salad, you will love this dip! Great for chicken or vegetables.

- dry measures
- measuring spoons
- small bowl
- mixing spoon

1.
Mayonnaise (or salad dressing)	⅓ cup	75 mL
Sour cream	⅓ cup	75 mL
Garlic powder	1 tsp.	5 mL
Lemon juice	1 tbsp.	15 mL

1. Combine the mayonnaise, sour cream, garlic powder and lemon juice in the bowl. Mix well. Chill in the refrigerator for 15 minutes to blend the flavors. Makes ⅔ cup (150 mL).

Sour Cream & Onion Dip chill

This is a tasty dip that complements chicken or vegetables.

- dry measures
- measuring spoons
- small bowl
- mixing spoon
- plastic wrap

1.
Sour cream	1 cup	250 mL
Plain yogurt	½ cup	125 mL
Minced onion flakes, crushed	2 tbsp.	30 mL
Beef bouillon powder	2½ tsp.	12 mL
Worcestershire sauce	¼ tsp.	1 mL

1. Combine all 5 ingredients in the bowl. Mix well. Cover with plastic wrap. Chill in the refrigerator for 1 hour to blend the flavors. Store any remaining dip in the refrigerator for up to 3 days. Makes 1½ cups (375 mL).

Dips & Spreads

Peanut Butter Pudding Dip chill

A great dipper for fruit, or chocolate or vanilla cookies.

1.	Peanut butter	⅓ cup	75 mL
	Milk	2 cups	500 mL
2.	Instant vanilla pudding powder, 4 serving size	1	1

- dry measures
- medium bowl
- mixing spoon
- liquid measures
- covered container

1. Cream the peanut butter in the bowl with the spoon. Add the milk, a bit at a time, stirring together until well mixed.

2. Add the instant pudding to the peanut butter mixture. Mix for 2 minutes. Chill in the refrigerator for about 5 minutes until slightly thickened. Store any remaining dip in the covered container for up to 4 days. Makes 2¾ cups (675 mL).

Pictured on page 108.

PEANUT BUTTER CHOCOLATE DIP: Use instant chocolate pudding powder instead of the instant vanilla pudding powder.

PEANUT BUTTER BUTTERSCOTCH DIP: Use instant butterscotch or caramel pudding powder instead of the instant vanilla pudding powder.

PEANUT BUTTER BANANA DIP: Use instant banana pudding powder instead of the instant vanilla pudding powder.

To keep fresh vegetables cold and crisp in your lunch, place ice cubes in a plastic sandwich bag with the vegetables. Close tightly with a twist tie. Wrap in another plastic sandwich bag and fasten again with another twist tie to prevent leakage.

Hot Tortilla Dip

Make this ahead and keep refrigerated. Reheat for lunch!

- dry measures
- small microwave-safe bowl
- sharp knife
- cutting board
- paper towel
- mixing spoon
- measuring spoons
- plastic wrap
- microwave oven
- oven mitts
- hot pad

1.	**Chunky salsa**	**¹/₂ cup**	**125 mL**
	Small tomato	**1**	**1**
2.	**Green onion, thinly sliced**	**1**	**1**
	Dried crushed chilies	**¹/₈ tsp.**	**0.5 mL**
3.	**Velveeta cheese, cut into small cubes**	**4 oz.**	**125 g**
4.	**Tortilla chips, for dipping**		
	Celery ribs, for dipping		

1. Place the salsa in the bowl. Cut the tomato in half on the cutting board. Gently squeeze over the paper towel to remove the seeds. Discard the seeds and juice. Dice the tomato into small pieces. Stir into the salsa.

2. Add the green onion and chilies. Cover with plastic wrap. Microwave on high (100%) for 1 minute.

3. Stir cheese into the warm salsa mixture. Microwave, uncovered, on high (100%) for 30 seconds. Stir well. Repeat until the cheese is all melted. Use the oven mitts to remove the bowl to the hot pad.

4. Serve with tortilla chips and celery ribs. Makes 1¹/₄ cups (300 mL).

Pictured on page 90.

You should never use metal pots or pans, tin foil, twist ties, lead crystal or melamine dishes or metal utensils in the microwave oven. All these products contain metal that will deflect the microwaves away from the food and could damage the microwave oven.

Dips & Spreads

Smoked Salmon Spread

Spread on bread, bagels or crackers.

1.			
Canned salmon, well drained	7½ oz.	213 g	
Plain spreadable cream cheese	⅓ cup	75 mL	
Finely chopped celery	1 tbsp.	15 mL	
Prepared horseradish	½ tsp.	2 mL	
Liquid smoke flavoring	⅛ tsp.	0.5 mL	
Onion powder	⅛ tsp.	0.5 mL	

- small bowl
- table fork
- dry measures
- measuring spoons
- mixing spoon
- covered container

1. Mash the salmon in the bowl with the fork. Add the remaining 5 ingredients. Mix well. Ready to use. Store any remaining spread in the container in the refrigerator for up to 3 days. Makes 1 cup (250 mL).

Pictured on page 125.

Pickly Tuna Spread

Spread on bread, bagels or crackers.

1.			
Canned tuna, drained and flaked	4¾ oz.	133 g	
Chopped dill pickle	½ cup	125 mL	
Chopped celery	½ cup	125 mL	
Mayonnaise (or salad dressing)	⅓ cup	75 mL	
Salt	⅛ tsp.	0.5 mL	
Pepper	⅛ tsp.	0.5 mL	

- dry measures
- measuring spoons
- small bowl
- mixing spoon
- covered container

1. Combine all 6 ingredients in the bowl. Mix well. Ready to use. Store any remaining spread in the container in the refrigerator for up to 3 days. Makes 2 cups (500 mL).

- measuring spoons
- medium bowl
- mixing spoon

Seedy Bread Spread

Use as a spread for bagels or any other kind of bread, or as a sandwich spread instead of mayonnaise.

1.			
Cream cheese, softened		4 oz.	125 g
Ranch (or your favorite creamy) dressing		2 tbsp.	30 mL
Finely chopped green, red or yellow pepper		2 tbsp.	30 mL
Finely grated carrot		1 tbsp.	15 mL
Finely chopped green onion		2 tbsp.	30 mL
Toasted sunflower seeds		1 tbsp.	15 mL
Cayenne pepper, sprinkle (optional)			
Salt		1/8 tsp.	0.5 mL
Pepper, sprinkle			

1. Combine all 9 ingredients in the bowl. Mix well. Makes 3/4 cup (175 mL).

1. Chili Fries, page 59
2. Fruity Waffles À La Mode, page 51
3. Easy Oven Omelet, page 49
4. Choco-O-Nut Spread, page 37

Dips & Spreads

Choc-O-Nut Spread

Spread on graham crackers, digestive biscuits or any other whole wheat or whole grain cracker.

1. | Smooth peanut butter | ½ cup | 125 mL |
    | Chocolate syrup | ⅓ cup | 75 mL |
    | Vanilla flavoring | 1 tsp. | 5 mL |

1. Combine all 3 ingredients in the bowl. Mix until smooth. Makes ¾ cup (175 mL).

Pictured on page 35.

- dry measures
- liquid measures
- measuring spoons
- small bowl
- mixing spoon

Jam & Cheese Spread

Try spreading on bagels, or roll up in flour tortillas.

1. | Plain spreadable cream cheese (½ cup, 125 mL) | ½ x 8 oz. | ½ x 227 g |
    | Thick jam (your favorite flavor) | ¼ cup | 60 mL |

1. Combine the cream cheese and jam in the bowl. Mix well. Makes ¾ cup (175 mL).

Pictured on page 125.

- dry measures
- small bowl
- table spoon

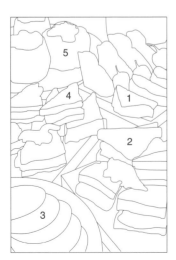

1. Hawaiian Grilled Cheese, page 116
2. Peanut Butter & Pickle Sandwich, 109
3. Snap Gingers, page 25
4. Ham & Cuke Sandwich, page 99
5. Tomato & Mozza Salad, page 93

Dips & Spreads 37

Chicken Thumbs hot

Good hot or cold. Great served with Dilly Pickle Dip, page 28, or Garlic Mustard Dip, page 29.

- baking sheet
- sharp knife
- cutting board
- measuring spoons
- medium bowl
- table fork
- mixing spoon
- dry measures
- plastic freezer bag
- oven mitts
- wire rack

1.	**Boneless, skinless chicken breast halves (about 1 lb., 454 g)**	**4**	**4**
2.	**Large egg**	**1**	**1**
	Milk	**2 tbsp.**	**30 mL**
	Seasoning salt	**½ tsp.**	**2 mL**
	Pepper, sprinkle		
3.	**Fine dry bread crumbs**	**¾ cup**	**175 mL**

1. Place the oven rack in the center position. Turn the oven on to 400°F (205°C). Grease the baking sheet. Cut the chicken crosswise, into 1 inch (2.5 cm) pieces, on the cutting board.

2. Combine the egg and milk in the bowl. Beat with the fork until frothy. Beat in the salt and pepper. Add the chicken. Stir to coat.

3. Put the bread crumbs into the bag. Remove 6 to 7 pieces of chicken from the egg mixture with the fork, and place into the bag of crumbs. Shake until coated. Place coated chicken on the baking sheet. Repeat for all the chicken pieces. Bake in the oven for 15 to 20 minutes. Use the oven mitts to remove the baking sheet to the wire rack. Makes about 30 pieces.

It is important to clean the cutting board and any utensils used to cut raw chicken, fish or beef very well in hot soapy water. This will eliminate any bacteria from spreading to other food.

Finger Foods

Nacho Skins (hot)

Zippy! Moist and very delicious. Save the scooped-out potato to fry tomorrow morning for breakfast.

1.	Medium baking potatoes, with peel	3	3
2.	Tub margarine	2 tbsp.	30 mL
	Salt	1/8 tsp.	0.5 mL
	Cayenne pepper, sprinkle		
3.	Canned green chilies, drained and blotted dry with paper towel	4 oz.	114 mL
	Grated Cheddar cheese	1 cup	250 mL
	Salsa	1/3 cup	75 mL
4.	Salsa, for dipping (optional)		
	Sour cream, for dipping (optional)		

- table fork
- oven mitts
- wire rack
- sharp knife
- cutting board
- table spoon
- 9 x 9 inch (22 x 22 cm) square baking pan
- measuring spoon
- custard cup
- microwave oven
- pastry brush
- dry measures
- small bowl

1. Place the oven rack in the center position. Turn the oven on to 425°F (220°C). Pierce the skin of each potato with the fork. Bake in the oven for 45 minutes. Use the oven mitts to remove the potatoes to the wire rack to cool. Cut each potato in half lengthwise on the cutting board. Cut each in half lengthwise again to make 4 wedges for each potato. Let cool enough to handle. Scoop out the potato from each wedge, leaving about 1/4 inch (6 mm) of potato on the skin. Place the wedges in the ungreased baking pan. Reduce the oven temperature to 350°F (175°C).

2. Place the margarine in the custard cup. Microwave on high (100%) for about 30 seconds. Stir in the salt and cayenne pepper. Brush the inside part of the potato skins with the margarine mixture.

3. Mix the green chilies with the cheese and salsa in the bowl. Spoon about 1 1/2 tbsp. (25 mL) of the mixture onto each potato skin wedge. Bake in the oven for 10 minutes until bubbling. Use the oven mitts to remove the pan to the wire rack.

4. Serve with salsa and sour cream. Makes 12 potato wedges.

Pictured on page 53.

- measuring spoons
- 9 × 9 inch (22 × 22 cm) square baking pan
- oven mitts
- wire rack
- plate
- microwave-safe plate
- microwave oven

Seeded Cheese

Cheese lovers will love these!

1.	Sesame seeds	2 tbsp.	30 mL
2.	Cheese (your favorite), cut into 10 sticks, ½ inch, (12 mm) thick, ½ inch (12 mm) wide and about 3 inches (7.5 cm) long	6 oz.	170 g

1. Place the oven rack in the upper position (second from the top). Turn the oven on to broil. Place the sesame seeds in the ungreased baking pan. Broil the seeds in the oven for about 3 minutes, shaking the pan occasionally using the oven mitts, until golden brown. Use the oven mitts to remove the pan to the wire rack. Put the warm seeds onto the plate.

2. Place the cheese on the microwave-safe plate. Microwave, uncovered, on high (100%) for 6 seconds until warm. Lightly press and roll the warmed cheese sticks in the seeds. Chill for 30 minutes. Makes about 10 cheese sticks.

Pictured on page 18.

- 6 wooden toothpicks

Ham & Melon Kabobs

Pack in a covered container to take to school.

1.	Thick ham slice (about 2 oz., 56 g), cut into six, ¾ inch (2 cm) cubes	1	1
	Small cantaloupe, cut into twelve, ¾ inch (2 cm) cubes	1	1

Continued on the next page.

1. Arrange 2 cubes of cantaloupe with 1 cube of ham in between on each toothpick. Makes 6 kabobs.

Pictured on page 107.

Variation: 6 pieces of shaved ham, rolled or folded into 1 inch (2.5 cm) pieces, may be substituted for the ham cubes. Toothpick will hold the shaved ham in place.

Spicy Chicken Fingers hot

Great warm or cold. Serve your favorite salsa with these, or try Dilly Pickle Dip, page 28.

1.	Boneless, skinless chicken breast halves (about 1 lb., 454 g)	4	4
2.	Large egg	1	1
	Milk	2 tbsp.	30 mL
3.	Cornmeal	²/₃ cup	150 mL
	Envelope taco seasoning mix (measure about 2¹/₂ tbsp., 37 mL)	¹/₂ × 1¹/₄ oz.	¹/₂ × 35 g
4.	Tub margarine	3 tbsp.	50 mL

- sharp knife
- cutting board
- measuring spoons
- small bowl
- table fork
- dry measures
- pie plate (or shallow dish)
- mixing spoon
- 9 × 13 inch (22 × 33 cm) oblong baking pan
- custard cup
- microwave oven
- oven mitts
- wire rack

1. Place the oven rack in the center position. Turn the oven on to 400°F (205°C). Cut each chicken breast into 4 pieces on the cutting board.

2. Beat the egg and milk together in the bowl with the fork until frothy.

3. Combine the cornmeal and taco seasoning in the pie plate. Stir. Dip each piece of chicken into the egg mixture and then roll in the cornmeal mixture until well coated. Place chicken in the ungreased baking pan.

4. Microwave the margarine in the custard cup on high (100%) for about 30 seconds until melted. Drizzle the chicken with the margarine. Bake in the oven for 15 minutes until crisp and golden. Use the oven mitts to remove the baking pan to the wire rack. Makes 16 pieces.

Pictured on the back cover.

Finger Foods

Salmon Cups (hot)

Makes a scrumptious lunch. Take these to school instead of the usual sandwich.

- muffin pan (for 8 muffins)
- measuring spoons
- small bowl
- mixing spoon
- oven mitts
- wire rack

1.	Canned salmon, well drained and mashed	7.5 oz.	213 g
	Finely chopped celery	2 tbsp.	30 mL
	Finely sliced green onion (or 2 tsp., 10 mL, dried chives)	1 tbsp.	15 mL
	Spreadable cream cheese	3 tbsp.	50 mL
	Large egg, fork-beaten	1	1
	Salt, sprinkle		
	Pepper, sprinkle		
	Dill weed (optional)	¼ tsp.	1 mL
2.	Refrigerator crescent-style rolls (tube of 8)	8 oz.	235 g

1. Place the oven rack in the center position. Turn the oven on to 350°F (175°C). Grease 8 muffin cups. Combine the first 8 ingredients in the bowl. Mix well.

2. Open the crescent rolls and separate into 8 triangles. Line the muffin cups with each triangle by placing the longest side of the triangle around the top edge of the muffin cup. Press all the edges together, forming the shape of the muffin cup. Put 2 tbsp. (30 mL) of the salmon mixture into each of the dough-lined cups. Bake for about 20 minutes until golden. Use the oven mitts to remove the muffin pan to the wire rack. Makes 8 salmon cups.

Pictured on the front cover.

Crispy Chicken Cracky (hot)

Try seasoned crackers such as vegetable-flavored or sour cream-flavored for a tasty treat. Serve hot or cold with Creamy Garlic Dip, page 30, Sour Cream & Onion Dip, page 30, or Garlic Mustard Dip, page 29.

1.	Boneless, skinless chicken breast halves (about 1 lb., 454 g)	4	4
2.	Tub margarine	¼ cup	60 mL
	Worcestershire sauce (optional)	1 tsp.	5 mL
	Salt	½ tsp.	2 mL
	Pepper	¼ tsp.	1 mL
3.	Soda (or your favorite) cracker crumbs, see Note	⅔ cup	150 mL

- baking sheet
- sharp knife
- cutting board
- medium bowl
- dry measures
- microwave-safe bowl
- microwave oven
- measuring spoons
- mixing spoon
- plastic freezer bag
- oven mitts
- wire rack

1. Place the oven rack in the center position. Turn the oven on to 400°F (205°C). Lightly grease the baking sheet. Cut each chicken breast into 6 chunks on the cutting board. Place in the medium bowl.

2. Microwave the margarine in the microwave-safe bowl on high (100%) for about 30 seconds until melted. Add the Worcestershire sauce, salt and pepper. Drizzle the margarine mixture over the chicken. Toss to coat.

3. Put the cracker crumbs into the bag. Put 3 or 4 pieces of chicken at a time in the bag of crumbs, shaking to coat well. Place the coated chicken on the baking sheet. Bake in the oven for 18 to 20 minutes until crisp and golden. Use the oven mitts to remove the baking sheet to the wire rack. Makes 24 chunks.

Note: To make crumbs, place the crackers in a plastic freezer bag and roll with a rolling pin.

Pictured on page 18.

Pepper-Corn Crackers hot

A soft and chewy cracker. A perfect addition to your lunch. These freeze well.

- dry measures
- measuring spoons
- medium bowl
- mixing spoon
- pastry blender
- baking sheet
- table fork
- oven mitts
- wire rack

1.

All-purpose flour	¾ cup	175 mL
Flakes of corn cereal	3 cups	750 mL
Baking powder	¼ tsp.	1 mL
Grated Cheddar (or Gouda or Edam or Monterey Jack) cheese	2 cups	500 mL
Hard margarine	½ cup	125 mL
Finely diced red pepper	½ cup	125 mL

2. Paprika, sprinkle

1. Turn the oven on to 350°F (175°C). Combine the flour, cereal and baking powder in the bowl. Add the cheese. Mix well. Cut in the margarine with the pastry blender until mixture looks crumbly with pieces no bigger than the size of a small pea. The mixture should almost want to stick together. Work with your hands until a stiff dough forms. Work in the red pepper.

2. Form 1½ tbsp. (25 mL) of dough into balls about 1 inch (2.5 cm) in diameter. Place the balls on the ungreased baking sheet. Flatten with the fork. Sprinkle with paprika. Bake on the center rack in the oven for 15 minutes until golden brown. Use the oven mitts to remove the baking sheet to the wire rack. Makes 40 crackers.

Pictured on page 54.

CHILI-CORN CRACKERS: Substitute a 4 oz. (114 mL) can of well-drained green chilies for the diced red pepper.

PEPPER-ONION CRACKERS: Add 2 tbsp. (30 mL) of thinly sliced green onion at the same time as you add the red pepper.

Easy Cheese Cups hot

Good warm or cold. These freeze well.

1.	Feta cheese, crumbled	½ cup	125 mL
	Creamed cottage cheese	½ cup	125 mL
2.	Plain (or herbed) spreadable cream cheese	3 tbsp.	50 mL
	Grated Parmesan (or Romano) cheese	1 tbsp.	15 mL
	Large egg, fork-beaten	1	1
	Dried whole oregano	⅛ tsp.	0.5 mL
	Dried sweet basil	⅛ tsp.	0.5 mL
	Parsley flakes	¼ tsp.	1 mL
	Garlic powder, sprinkle		
	Lemon juice	½ tsp.	2 mL
3.	Refrigerator crescent-style rolls (tube of 8)	8 oz.	235 g

- muffin pan (for 8 muffins)
- dry measures
- small bowl
- table fork
- measuring spoons
- electric mixer
- oven mitts
- wire rack

1. Place the oven rack in the center position. Turn the oven on to 350°F (175°C). Grease 8 muffin cups. Mash the feta cheese and cottage cheese together with the fork in the bowl.

2. Add the next 8 ingredients. Beat on medium speed until smooth. Makes 1 cup (250 mL).

3. Open the crescent rolls and separate into 8 triangles. Line the muffin cups with each triangle by placing the longest side of the triangle around the top edge of the muffin cup. Press all the edges together, forming the shape of the muffin cup. Divide the creamed filling evenly among the 8 dough-lined cups. Bake in the oven for 20 to 25 minutes. Use the oven mitts to remove the muffin pan to the wire rack. Makes 8 cheese cups.

Simple Sloppy Joes

Serve over toast, toasted bun halves, or inside slightly hollowed-out buns.

- non-stick frying pan
- mixing spoon
- colander
- measuring spoons
- dry measures

1.	Lean ground beef	1 lb.	454 g
2.	Condensed tomato soup	10 oz.	284 mL
	Ketchup	2 tbsp.	30 mL
	Prepared mustard	1 tbsp.	15 mL
	Sweet pickle relish	¼ cup	60 mL

1. Scramble-fry the ground beef in the frying pan over medium heat until browned and no longer pink. Drain off fat.

2. Stir in the next 4 ingredients. Simmer, uncovered, over low heat for 20 minutes. Makes 2 cups (500 mL).

Easy Chili

Chili is always better the next day when all the flavors have come together.

- non-stick frying pan
- mixing spoon
- measuring spoons

1.	Lean ground beef	1 lb.	454 g
	Medium onion, chopped	1	1
	Large celery rib, sliced	1	1
2.	All-purpose flour	2 tbsp.	30 mL
	Canned chopped stewed tomatoes, with juice	14 oz.	398 mL
	Garlic powder	¼ tsp.	1 mL
	Canned kidney beans, drained	14 oz.	398 mL
	Chili powder	1 tbsp.	15 mL
	Granulated sugar	2 tsp.	10 mL
	Paprika	1 tsp.	5 mL
	Salt	½ tsp.	2 mL

Continued on the next page.

1. Scramble-fry the ground beef with the onion and celery in the frying pan over medium heat until the beef is no longer pink and the vegetables are tender-crisp.

2. Sprinkle the surface of the beef mixture with the flour. Stir for 1 minute. Add the remaining 7 ingredients. Bring to a boil. Cover. Simmer over low heat for 30 minutes, stirring several times. Makes 5¾ cups (1.4 L).

Pictured on page 54.

Spaghetti One-Dish

Nice and thick. Even the pasta is cooked in the sauce. A one-dish meal.

1.	Lean ground beef	½ lb.	225 g
	Medium onion, chopped	1	1
	Medium green pepper, chopped	½	½
2.	Canned sliced mushrooms, with liquid	10 oz.	284 mL
	Canned stewed tomatoes, with juice	14 oz.	398 mL
	Tomato sauce	7½ oz.	213 mL
	Granulated sugar	1 tsp.	5 mL
3.	Uncooked spaghetti, broken-up	4 oz.	113 g
	Grated Parmesan cheese	1 tbsp.	15 mL

- frying pan with lid
- mixing spoon
- measuring spoons
- small bowl

1. Scramble-fry the ground beef with the onion and green pepper in the frying pan or Dutch oven over medium heat until the beef is browned and the vegetables are soft.

2. Add the mushrooms, tomatoes, tomato sauce and sugar. Cover. Bring to a boil.

3. Add the spaghetti. Stir well. Cover. Reduce the heat to medium-low. Cook for 10 minutes. Stir in the cheese just before serving. Makes 5½ cups (1.3 L), enough for 2 servings.

Spicy Taco Pie (hot)

A great all-in-one meal to do on weekends. Burst of Mexican flavors with a golden brown biscuit crust.

- 10 inch (25 cm) glass pie plate
- non-stick frying pan
- mixing spoon
- measuring spoons
- dry measures
- liquid measures
- medium bowl
- waxed paper
- rolling pin
- ruler
- table spoon
- oven mitts
- wire rack

1.	Lean ground beef	1 lb.	454 g
	Canned brown beans in tomato sauce	14 oz.	398 mL
	Envelope taco seasoning mix	1¼ oz.	35 g
2.	Cornmeal	1 tbsp.	15 mL
3.	Biscuit mix	2 cups	500 mL
	Milk	⅔ cup	150 mL
4.	Grated Monterey Jack cheese	½ cup	125 mL
	Grated Cheddar cheese	½ cup	125 mL
	Crushed corn chips	½ cup	125 mL
	Shredded lettuce	1 cup	250 mL
	Medium tomato, chopped	1	1
	Green onion, thinly sliced (optional)	1	1
	Sour cream	½ cup	125 mL

1. Place the oven rack in the center position. Turn the oven on to 400°F (205°C). Grease the pie plate. Scramble-fry the ground beef in the frying pan over medium heat until no longer pink. Stir in the beans and taco seasoning. Reduce the heat to low. Simmer, uncovered, for 5 minutes.

2. Sprinkle cornmeal in the bottom of the pie plate.

3. Combine the biscuit mix and milk in the bowl. Stir until it forms a ball. Knead dough 7 or 8 times on a lightly floured working surface. Roll out on waxed paper into a 12 inch (30 cm) circle. Turn dough over into the pie plate. Peel off the waxed paper. Press dough lightly to form a shell. Spoon the beef mixture into the shell. Bake in the oven for 12 minutes until the crust is golden. Use the oven mitts to remove the pie plate to the wire rack.

4. Sprinkle with both cheeses, corn chips, lettuce, tomato and green onion. Place dollops of sour cream on top. Cuts into 6 wedges.

Pictured on page 53.

Easy Oven Omelet hot

Great with lots of cheese.

1.	Large eggs	6	6
	Skim evaporated milk	13½ oz.	385 mL
	All-purpose flour	1 tbsp.	15 mL
	Salt	¼ tsp.	1 mL
2.	Grated Cheddar (or Swiss) cheese	1½ cups	375 mL
	Green onions, sliced	2	2
	Medium tomato, chopped	1	1

1. Place the oven rack in the center position. Turn the oven on to 325°F (160°C). Grease the pie plate. Beat the eggs, milk, flour and salt together on medium speed in the bowl.

2. Sprinkle the remaining 3 ingredients in the bottom of the pie plate. Pour the egg mixture gently over top. Bake in the oven for 60 to 65 minutes until the knife inserted into the center of the omelet comes out clean. Use the oven mitts to remove the pie plate to the wire rack. Serves 4 to 6.

Pictured on page 35.

- deep 9 inch (22 cm) pie plate (or 1 quart, 1 L, casserole dish)
- measuring spoons
- medium bowl
- electric mixer
- dry measures
- table knife
- oven mitts
- wire rack

Eggs In Ham Cups hot

Fun way to serve ham and eggs.

1.	Round deli ham (or bologna) slices	4	4
2.	Large eggs	4	4

1. Place the oven rack in the bottom position. Turn the oven on to 350°F (175°C). Grease 4 muffin cups in the muffin pan. Fit 1 ham slice into each of the 4 muffin cups to form a shell.

2. Break 1 egg into each of the ham-lined muffin cups. Bake in the oven for 12 to 15 minutes. Use the oven mitts to remove the muffin pan to the wire rack. Remove the ham cups to the plate. Makes 4 ham cups.

- muffin pan
- oven mitts
- wire rack
- serving plate

Kid Kwik Stir-Fry

A full meal in one bowl!

- liquid measures
- measuring spoons
- mixing spoon
- small cup (or bowl)
- non-stick frying pan with lid
- dry measures
- hot pad

1.	Cold water	½ cup	125 mL
	Cornstarch	2 tsp.	10 mL
	Soy sauce	2 tsp.	10 mL
	Garlic powder, sprinkle		
2.	Cooking oil	1 tsp.	5 mL
	Chopped fresh broccoli (or cauliflower)	½ cup	125 mL
	Thinly sliced carrot	¼ cup	60 mL
	Medium fresh mushrooms, sliced	2	2
	Diced cooked roast beef (or pork or chicken)	½ cup	125 mL
3.	Dry steam-fried noodles	½ cup	125 mL

1. Stir the cold water, cornstarch, soy sauce and garlic powder together in the cup. Set aside.

2. Heat the cooking oil in the frying pan over medium-high heat. Stir-fry the next 4 ingredients in the hot oil for 4 to 5 minutes. Quickly stir the cornstarch mixture again and add to the vegetables in the frying pan. Cover. Cook until bubbling, thickened and clear.

3. Stir in the noodles. Cover and remove the frying pan from the heat to the hot pad. Let stand for 3 minutes. Makes 1¾ cups (425 mL), enough for 1 serving.

Fruit Waffles À La Mode (hot)

As delicious as cherry pie. Use a variety of pie fillings for different tastes. Try peach or raisin. Gets top marks for presentation and eye appeal.

1.	Frozen plain (or buttermilk) waffles	2	2
2.	Canned cherry pie filling	½ cup	125 mL
3.	Small scoops of vanilla ice cream	2	2

- baking sheet
- dry measures
- table spoon
- oven mitts
- wire rack
- pancake lifter
- luncheon plates
- ice-cream scoop

1. Place the oven rack in the center position. Turn the oven on to 350°F (175°C). Place both waffles on the ungreased baking sheet.

2. Spoon ¼ cup (60 mL) of pie filling onto each waffle. Bake in the oven for 20 minutes until the pie filling is hot and bubbling and the waffle is crisp. Use the oven mitts to remove the baking sheet to the wire rack. Use the pancake lifter to place the waffles on the plates.

3. Top each hot waffle with 1 scoop of ice cream. Makes 2 waffles.

Pictured on page 35.

Did you know?

If you have a microwave oven available at lunchtime, you can freeze individual servings of some finger foods or hot lunches recipes. You will be able to put these in your lunch directly from the frozen state and heat them up in the microwave oven when it's time.

Corn Cakes

Much like a corn fritter.

1.	Large eggs	2	2
	Seasoning salt	½ tsp.	2 mL
2.	All-purpose flour	⅓ cup	75 mL
	Baking powder	1 tsp.	5 mL
3.	Canned kernel corn, drained	12 oz.	341 mL
	Grated Cheddar cheese	⅓ cup	75 mL
4.	Cooking oil	2 tbsp.	30 mL

- measuring spoons
- medium bowl
- whisk
- dry measures
- mixing spoon
- non-stick frying pan
- pancake lifter

1. Beat the eggs and seasoning salt together in the medium bowl with the whisk.

2. Add the flour and baking powder. Whisk until smooth.

3. Add the corn and cheese. Stir to mix.

4. Heat the cooking oil in the frying pan over medium heat until hot. Drop the batter by rounded tablespoonfuls into the frying pan. Cook until golden. Turn the corn cakes over with the pancake lifter to cook the other side. Cook until golden. Makes about twelve 3 inch (7.5 cm) corn cakes.

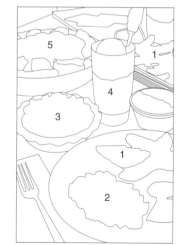

1. Nacho Skins, page 39
2. Creamy Macaroni & Cheese, page 60
3. Bean & Tomato Salad, page 94
4. Lemon Cola Float, page 13
5. Spicy Taco Pie, page 48

Quick Bread "Sandwich" hot

Cheese adds a nice flavor to the biscuit crust.

1.			
Biscuit mix	1½ cups	375 mL
Grated sharp Cheddar cheese	1 cup	250 mL
Water	¾ cup	175 mL
Dry mustard	1 tsp.	5 mL
2.			
Shaved or chopped ham (or other deli meat)	8 oz.	225 g
Grated sharp Cheddar cheese	1 cup	250 mL
Green onions, sliced (optional)	2	2
Chopped green or red pepper	¼ cup	60 mL

1. Place the oven rack in the center position. Turn the oven on to 350°F (175°C). Grease the pie plate. Combine the biscuit mix, first amount of cheese, water and dry mustard in the bowl. Mix well.

2. Spread ½ of the batter in the pie plate. Cover with the ham, second amount of cheese, green onion and green pepper. Spread the remaining ½ of the batter over the top as well as you can. Bake, uncovered, in the oven for 25 to 30 minutes. Use the oven mitts to remove the pie plate to the wire rack. Serves 6 to 8.

- 9 inch (22 cm) pie plate
- dry measures
- liquid measures
- measuring spoons
- medium bowl
- mixing spoon
- table spoon
- oven mitts
- wire rack

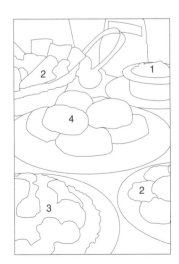

1. Easy Chili, page 46
2. Pepper-Corn Crackers, page 44
3. Fruity Banana Meatballs, page 66
4. Pizza Pinwheels, page 80

Hot Lunches 55

Quick Turkey Loaf hot

This is perfect for sandwich meat. Slices well when cold. Freeze individual slices for your lunch.

- 9 × 5 × 3 inch (22 × 12 × 7 cm) loaf pan
- dry measures
- measuring spoons
- blender
- large bowl
- mixing spoon
- oven mitts
- wire rack

1.	Large egg	1	1
	Ketchup	⅓ cup	75 mL
	Seasoning salt	1½ tsp.	7 mL
	Pepper	⅛ tsp.	0.5 mL
	Small onion, cut into chunks	1	1
	Large carrot, peeled and cut into chunks	1	1
	Large celery rib, cut into chunks	1	1
2.	Lean ground chicken (or turkey)	1½ lbs.	680 g
	Large flake (old-fashioned) rolled oats	⅔ cup	150 mL

1. Place the oven rack in the center position. Turn the oven on to 350°F (175°C). Grease the loaf pan. Combine the egg, ketchup, seasoning salt and pepper in the blender. Process until smooth. While blender is processing, gradually add the onion, carrot and celery, a few at a time, through the opening in the lid. Process until almost smooth. There will be some very small chunks of vegetable remaining.

2. Put the ground turkey into the bowl. Pour the vegetable mixture over. Mix well. Stir in the rolled oats and let stand for 10 minutes. Pack into the loaf pan. Bake in the oven for 1¼ hours. Use the oven mitts to remove the pan to the wire rack. Let stand for 5 minutes. Cuts into 10 to 12 slices.

Pictured on page 126.

Creamy Beef 'N' Pasta

Much like stroganoff. Easy because it's made in one dish.

1.	Lean ground beef	1 lb.	454 g
	Medium onion, chopped	1	1
2.	Seasoning salt	1 tsp.	5 mL
	Pepper	⅛ tsp.	0.5 mL
	Beef bouillon powder	1 tbsp.	15 mL
	Hot water	1½ cups	375 mL
	Canned sliced mushrooms, with liquid	10 oz.	284 mL
	Condensed cream of mushroom soup	10 oz.	284 mL
	Uncooked elbow macaroni (or small shell pasta)	1 cup	250 mL
3.	Sour cream	½ cup	125 mL

- large frying pan with lid
- mixing spoon
- measuring spoons
- liquid measures
- dry measures
- oven mitts
- hot pad

1. Scramble-fry the ground beef in the frying pan over medium heat for about 3 minutes. Add the onion. Scramble-fry until the beef is browned and the onion is soft. Drain off fat.

2. Sprinkle the beef mixture with the seasoning salt, pepper and bouillon powder. Pour in the hot water, mushrooms and mushroom soup. Bring mixture to a boil. Stir in the macaroni. Cover and reduce the heat to medium-low. Cook for 15 minutes, stirring once or twice until the macaroni is tender.

3. Use the oven mitts to remove the frying pan to the hot pad. Stir in the sour cream. Makes 6 cups (1.5 L), enough for 2 servings.

Doctored Beans

A great source of protein. A delicious old-fashioned favorite.

- dry measures
- measuring spoons
- 1 quart (1 L) microwave-safe dish with lid
- microwave oven
- mixing spoon

1.	Canned baked brown beans in molasses (or in tomato sauce)	14 oz.	398 mL
	Diced cooked ham	½ cup	125 mL
	Ketchup	1 tsp.	5 mL
	Prepared mustard	1 tsp.	5 mL
	Brown sugar, packed	1 tsp.	5 mL
	Onion powder	⅛ tsp.	0.5 mL

1. Combine all 6 ingredients in the dish. Cover. Microwave on high (100%) for 2 minutes. Stir. Cover. Microwave for 2 minutes. Let stand for 2 minutes before serving. Makes 1¾ cups (425 mL).

Macaroni & Cottage Cheese

A new twist to an old favorite.

- liquid measures
- measuring spoons
- medium saucepan
- dry measures
- mixing spoon
- colander
- frying pan

1.	Water	4 cups	1 L
	Salt	1 tsp.	5 mL
	Uncooked elbow macaroni (or small shell pasta)	1½ cups	375 mL
2.	Tub margarine	2 tsp.	10 mL
	Finely chopped onion	⅓ cup	75 mL
	Simulated bacon bits (or 1 bacon slice, cooked crisp and crumbled)	1 tbsp.	15 mL
	Creamed cottage cheese	1¼ cups	300 mL
	Salt, sprinkle		
	Pepper, sprinkle		

Continued on the next page.

1. Bring the water and first amount of salt to a boil in the saucepan. Add the macaroni. Cook, stirring occasionally, for 7 to 9 minutes until just tender. Drain pasta in the colander. Rinse with hot water and drain again. Return the pasta to the saucepan. Cover to keep warm.

2. Melt the margarine in the frying pan. Add the onion and sauté until soft and golden. Add the bacon bits. Pour the onion mixture over the pasta. Stir in the cottage cheese. Sprinkle with the second amount of salt and pepper. Makes 4 cups (1 L).

Pictured on page 89.

Chili Fries (hot)

Just like the ones you would get in a fast-food restaurant—only better!

1.	Lean ground beef	1 lb.	454 g
	Chopped onion	1 cup	250 mL
	Finely chopped celery	2 cups	500 mL
2.	All-purpose flour	1 tbsp.	15 mL
	Canned kidney beans, drained	14 oz.	398 mL
	Seasoning salt	1 tsp.	5 mL
	Pepper	1/8 tsp.	0.5 mL
	Chili powder	1 1/2 tsp.	7 mL
	Tomato sauce	7 1/2 oz.	213 mL
	Ketchup	1/4 cup	60 mL
3.	Frozen french fries (1/2 × 2.2 lbs., 1/2 × 1 kg., package)	4 cups	1 L

- non-stick frying pan
- mixing spoon
- dry measures
- measuring spoons
- 9 × 13 inch (22 × 33 cm) oblong baking pan
- oven mitts
- wire rack

1. Place the oven rack in the center position. Turn the oven on to 425°F (220°C). Scramble-fry the ground beef in the frying pan over medium heat for 3 minutes. Add the onion and celery. Scramble-fry until the beef is no longer pink and the onion is soft.

2. Sprinkle with the flour. Stir well. Add the next 6 ingredients. Mix well. Bring to a boil. Pour into the ungreased pan.

3. Top with the french fries. Bake in the oven for 25 to 30 minutes. Use the oven mitts to remove the pan to the wire rack. Serves 6.

Pictured on page 35.

Creamy Macaroni & Cheese

Make this delicious homemade version.

1.	Tub margarine	1 tbsp.	15 mL
	Chopped onion	¼ cup	60 mL
2.	All-purpose flour	1½ tbsp.	25 mL
	Skim evaporated milk	1 cup	250 mL
	Grated Cheddar cheese	½ cup	125 mL
	Process Cheddar cheese slices	2	2
	Salt	¼ tsp.	1 mL
	Pepper, sprinkle		
	Dry mustard (or paprika), optional	¾ tsp.	4 mL
3.	Water	8 cups	2 L
	Elbow macaroni (or small shell pasta)	1 cup	250 mL

- measuring spoons
- small saucepan
- dry measures
- 2 mixing spoons
- liquid measures
- large saucepan
- colander

1. Melt the margarine over medium heat in the small saucepan. Sauté the onion until soft.

2. Stir in the flour. Gradually add the milk, stirring constantly, until boiling. Stir in the cheeses, salt, pepper and dry mustard. Stir until the cheese is melted. Remove from the heat.

3. Measure the water into the large saucepan. Bring to a boil. Stir in the macaroni. Cook for 5 to 6 minutes until the pasta is just tender. Drain in the colander. Place in the saucepan. Add the cheese sauce to the pasta. Stir well. Makes 4 cups (1 L).

Note: This can be made ahead of time and rewarmed in a 350°F (175°C) oven in a 1 quart (1 L) casserole dish for 30 to 40 minutes.

Pictured on page 53.

Two-Potato Pancakes

These are delicious and a nice change from the usual lunch.

1.	Medium baking potatoes, peeled and grated	2	2
	Chopped onion	⅓ cup	75 mL
	All-purpose flour	1 tbsp.	15 mL
	Large egg, fork-beaten	1	1
	Salt	¼ tsp.	1 mL
	Pepper, sprinkle		
2.	Cooking oil	1½ tsp.	7 mL
3.	Applesauce (or sour cream), for garnish		

- colander
- 4 paper towels
- dry measures
- measuring spoons
- medium bowl
- mixing spoon
- frying pan
- pancake lifter

1. Rinse the grated potato with cold water in the colander. Dry between the paper towels. Combine the potato with the next 5 ingredients in the bowl. Mix well.

2. Heat the cooking oil in the frying pan over medium heat. Drop heaping ¼ cup (60 mL) measures of potato mixture into the frying pan, forming individual potato pancakes. Cook for 5 minutes until golden brown. Turn the pancakes over with the pancake lifter to cook the other side. Cook for 5 minutes until golden brown.

3. Serve with applesauce or sour cream. Makes 10 pancakes.

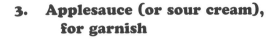
Did you know?

When dry bread crumbs are needed in a recipe, use stale (or 2 day-old) white or whole wheat bread. Using fresh bread will make the crumbs soggy. Remove the crusts from the bread. Cut or break into pieces then blend or process until fine crumbs form. Store bread crumbs in an airtight container or in a sealable plastic bag. Bread crumbs can also be frozen.

- sharp knife
- cutting board
- measuring spoons
- small bowl
- mixing spoon
- microwave-safe plate
- microwave oven

Stuffed Smokie

Pack the stuffing well. Nice spicy taste.

1.	Smokie sausage	1	1
2.	Fine dry bread crumbs	1 tbsp.	15 mL
	Tub margarine, melted	½ tsp.	2 mL
	Water	1 tsp.	5 mL
	Grated Cheddar cheese	1 tbsp.	15 mL

1. Split the sausage lengthwise, part way through but not completely, on the cutting board.

2. Combine the remaining 4 ingredients in the bowl. Mix well. Pack the mixture into the split opening of the sausage and on top. Place on the plate. Microwave on high (100%) for 1 minute. Makes 1 serving.

- measuring spoons
- large frying pan with lid
- mixing spoon
- liquid measures
- dry measures
- small cup

Pineapple Chicken & Rice

Sweet and sour taste, with chunky texture.

1.	Cooking oil	1 tsp.	5 mL
	Lean ground chicken	1 lb.	454 g
	Small onion, chopped	1	1
	Large celery rib, sliced	1	1
	Medium carrots, sliced	2	2
	Canned pineapple chunks, with juice	14 oz.	398 mL
	Hot water	2 cups	500 mL
	Chicken bouillon powder	1 tbsp.	15 mL
	Uncooked long grain white rice	¾ cup	175 mL
	Chopped green or red pepper	½ cup	125 mL
2.	Brown sugar, packed	2 tbsp.	30 mL
	White vinegar	2 tbsp.	30 mL
	Ketchup	1 tbsp.	15 mL
	Soy sauce	2 tsp.	10 mL

Continued on the next page.

1. Heat the cooking oil in the frying pan over medium heat. Scramble-fry the ground chicken for 2 to 3 minutes. Add the onion, celery and carrot. Scramble-fry for 5 minutes until the chicken is no longer pink. Stir in the pineapple chunks with juice, hot water and bouillon powder. Bring to a boil and stir in the rice. Cover and simmer over medium-low heat for 15 minutes. Stir in the green pepper. Cover. Cook for 5 minutes until the rice is tender.

2. Combine the next 4 ingredients in the cup. Stir into the chicken rice mixture. Makes 7 cups (1.75 L).

Broccoli 'N' Rice

Get your starch, vegetable and protein all together in this dish.

1.			
Uncooked instant white rice	½ cup	125 mL
Minced onion flakes	1 tbsp.	15 mL
Water	½ cup	125 mL
Chopped fresh broccoli	2 cups	500 mL
Condensed cream of celery soup	10 oz.	284 mL
Salt	½ tsp.	2 mL
Pepper, sprinkle		
2. Process Cheddar cheese slices, cut into small pieces	4	4

1. Layer the first 7 ingredients, in order given, in the casserole dish. Cover. Microwave on high (100%) for 5 minutes. Stir. Cover and cook for 5 minutes. Use the oven mitts to remove the casserole dish to the hot pad.

2. Stir the cheese into the rice mixture. Cover. Let stand for 2 minutes. Stir. Makes 5 cups (1.25 L).

- dry measures
- measuring spoons
- liquid measures
- 1 quart (1 L) casserole dish
- microwave oven
- mixing spoon
- oven mitts
- hot pad

Mexican Potato Casserole hot

Very tasty! Make ahead and reheat when you're ready for lunch.

- 1½ quart (1.5 L) casserole dish
- measuring spoons
- custard cup
- microwave oven
- mixing spoon
- sharp knife
- non-stick frying pan
- dry measures
- table spoon
- oven mitts
- wire rack

1.	Medium potatoes, with peel, cut into bite-size chunks	3	3
2.	Tub margarine	2 tbsp.	30 mL
	Envelope taco seasoning mix (measure about 2½ tbsp., 37 mL)	½ × 1¼ oz.	½ × 35 g
3.	Lean ground beef	½ lb.	225 g
	Chopped onion	¼ cup	60 mL
	Salsa	1 cup	250 mL
	Chopped green pepper	½ cup	125 mL
4.	Grated Monterey Jack cheese	1 cup	250 mL

1. Place the oven rack in the center position. Turn the oven on to 425°F (220°C). Lightly grease the casserole dish. Place the potatoes in the casserole dish.

2. Place the margarine in the custard cup. Microwave on high (100%) for 30 to 50 seconds until melted. Stir in the taco seasoning. Pour over the potatoes. Stir to coat well. Bake, uncovered, in the oven for 40 minutes. Stir. Bake for about 10 minutes until the potatoes feel soft when poked with the knife.

3. Scramble-fry the ground beef in the frying pan over medium-high heat for 3 minutes. Add the onion. Scramble-fry until the beef is no longer pink and the onion is soft. Remove from the heat. Drain off fat. Stir in the salsa and green pepper.

4. Spoon the beef mixture over the potato in the casserole dish. Top with the cheese. Bake, uncovered, in the oven for 10 minutes. Use the oven mitts to remove the casserole dish to the wire rack. Serves 4.

Broccoli-Sauced Potatoes (hot)

Thick and creamy broccoli sauce in every mouthful.

1.	Medium potatoes, with peel	4	4
	Cooking oil	1 tsp.	5 mL
2.	Chopped broccoli, fresh or frozen	2 cups	500 mL
	Water	½ cup	125 mL
3.	Tub margarine	2 tbsp.	30 mL
	Chopped onion	¼ cup	60 mL
	All-purpose flour	3 tbsp.	50 mL
	Milk	1 cup	250 mL
4.	Process Swiss cheese slices (or your favorite), cut into small pieces	4	4
	Ground nutmeg, sprinkle		
	Seasoning salt	½ tsp.	2 mL
	Pepper, sprinkle		

GET READY GET SET!

- table fork
- measuring spoons
- sharp knife
- oven mitts
- wire rack
- dry measures
- liquid measures
- medium saucepan
- colander
- mixing spoon
- luncheon plates

1. Place the oven rack in the center position. Turn the oven on to 425°F (220°C). Wash the potatoes well. Poke 3 or 4 times with the fork. Coat your hands with the cooking oil and rub the potatoes all over. Bake in the oven for 45 to 50 minutes until tender when pierced with the knife. Use the oven mitts to remove the potatoes to the wire rack.

2. Put the broccoli into the water in the saucepan. Bring to a boil. Reduce the heat to low. Cover and simmer for 5 minutes until tender. Remove from the heat. Drain well in the colander. Set aside.

3. Melt the margarine in the same saucepan over medium heat. Sauté the onion until soft. Sprinkle the flour over the onion. Mix well. Gradually stir in the milk, stirring continually, until the sauce is boiling and thickened.

4. Stir the cheese into the hot sauce. Add nutmeg, seasoning salt and pepper. Stir until the cheese is melted. Add the broccoli. Stir. Cut the potatoes in half and place on individual plates. Fluff up the insides with the fork. Spoon about ¼ cup (60 mL) of broccoli sauce over each potato half. Makes 2½ cups (625 mL) broccoli sauce, enough for 8 potato halves.

Pictured on page 71.

Fruity Banana Meatballs: hot

The fruit sauce is great served over rice. This is a delicious hot lunch.

- 2½ quart (2.5 L) casserole dish
- dry measures
- measuring spoons
- medium bowl
- mixing spoon
- small bowl
- sharp knife
- cutting board
- oven mitts
- wire rack
- serving platter

1.	Ground pork and beef mix (or ½ lb., 225 g, each of ground pork and ground beef)	1 lb.	454 g
	Finely chopped onion	⅓ cup	75 mL
	Seasoning salt	½ tsp.	2 mL
	Garlic powder	⅛ tsp.	0.5 mL
	Large egg, fork-beaten	1	1
	Fine dry bread crumbs	⅓ cup	75 mL
2.	Canned fruit cocktail, with juice	14 oz.	398 mL
	Lemon juice	2 tbsp.	30 mL
	Brown sugar, packed	3 tbsp.	50 mL
	Cornstarch	1 tbsp.	15 mL
	Curry powder	½ tsp.	2 mL
	Firm medium bananas, peeled	2	2
3.	Hot cooked rice (or couscous)	4 cups	1 L

1. Place the oven rack in the center position. Turn the oven on to 400°F (205°C). Grease the casserole dish. Combine the first 6 ingredients in the medium bowl. Mix well. Form into 1 inch (2.5 cm) balls. Place in a single layer in the casserole dish. Bake, uncovered, in the oven for 20 minutes. Drain off fat.

2. Combine the next 5 ingredients in the small bowl. Cut the banana into ½ inch (12 mm) thick slices on the cutting board. Stir into the fruit cocktail mixture. Pour over the meatballs. Cover. Bake for 30 minutes until bubbling and the banana is softened, but not mushy. Use the oven mitts to remove the casserole dish to the wire rack.

3. Arrange the rice on the platter. Spoon the meatballs and sauce over the rice to serve. Makes about 24 meatballs and 2⅓ cups (575 mL) fruit sauce.

Pictured on page 54.

Poutine

Pronounced poo-TIN. Try this delicious French-Canadian dish today!

1.	**Frozen french fries** (½ x **2.2 lbs.**, ½ x **1 kg**, package)	**4 cups**	**1 L**
2.	**Water**	**1 cup**	**250 mL**
	All-purpose flour	**2 tbsp.**	**30 mL**
	Beef bouillon powder	**2 tsp.**	**10 mL**
	Onion powder	**¼ tsp.**	**1 mL**
	Seasoning salt	**¼ tsp.**	**1 mL**
	Pepper, sprinkle		
	Liquid gravy browner (optional)		
3.	**Grated mozzarella cheese**	**1 cup**	**250 mL**

- 9 × 13 inch (22 × 33 cm) oblong baking pan
- oven mitts
- wire rack
- pancake lifter
- liquid measures
- measuring spoons
- jar with lid
- small saucepan
- mixing spoon
- dry measures

1. Place the oven rack in the bottom position. Turn the oven on to 450°F (230°C). Place the frozen fries in the ungreased pan. Bake for 10 minutes. Use the oven mitts to remove the pan to the wire rack. Mix the fries, turning them over with the pancake lifter. Return the pan to the oven. Bake for 10 minutes. Use the oven mitts to remove the pan to the wire rack.

2. Put the water and flour into the jar. Fit the lid on tightly. Shake the jar until flour mixture appears to be smooth. Pour the mixture into the saucepan. Add the bouillon powder, onion powder, seasoning salt and pepper. Stir over medium heat until the sauce is bubbling and slightly thickened. Add the gravy browner if desired. Pour the sauce over the hot fries in the pan.

3. Top with the cheese. Bake for 2 minutes until the cheese is melted. Serves 4.

Ham Stacks

Very quick and easy. The sauce is tasty with a hint of cloves.

- paper towel
- liquid measures
- measuring spoons
- pie plate (or shallow dish)
- mixing spoon
- frying pan
- pancake lifter
- serving plate

1.	**Maraschino cherries**	4	4
	Canned sliced pineapple rings, drained, ½ cup (125 mL) juice reserved	4	4
2.	**Reserved pineapple juice**		
	Brown sugar, packed	2 tbsp.	30 mL
	Ground ginger	¼ tsp.	1 mL
	Ground cloves, sprinkle		
	Baked round ham slices, cut ¼ inch (6 mm) thick (about 10 oz., 285 g)	4	4
3.	**Tub margarine**	1 tsp.	5 mL
4.	**Cornstarch**	2 tsp.	10 mL

1. Dry the cherries and pineapple slices on the paper towel.

2. Stir the pineapple juice, sugar, ginger and cloves together in the pie plate. Place the ham slices in the juice mixture, turning each slice several times to coat.

3. Melt ½ tsp. (2 mL) of the margarine in the frying pan over medium heat. Remove the ham from the juice mixture and place in the frying pan. Cook the ham for 5 minutes until golden. Turn the ham over with the pancake lifter to cook the other side. Cook for 5 minutes until golden. Remove the ham slices to the serving plate. Melt the remaining ½ tsp. (2 mL) of the margarine in the frying pan. Cook the pineapple slices for 3 minutes on each side. Place 1 pineapple slice on top of each ham slice. Place a cherry in the center of each pineapple slice. Keep warm.

4. Stir the cornstarch into the remaining juice mixture in the pie plate. Pour into the frying pan. Stir until the sauce is bubbling and thickened. Drizzle 1 tbsp. (15 mL) of the sauce over each decorated ham slice. Serves 4.

Pictured on page 71.

Hot Lunches

Stuffed Potato Boats

These potato boats can be wrapped and frozen.
Microwave on high (100%) for one minute if the potato is
thawed, or microwave, covered, on high (100%) for two
and one-half to three minutes if frozen.

1.	Medium potato, with peel	1	1
2.	Tub margarine	2 tsp.	10 mL
	Onion salt	1/4 tsp.	1 mL
	Pepper	1/16 tsp.	0.5 mL
	Grated Parmesan cheese	1 tbsp.	15 mL
	Sour cream	1/4 cup	60 mL
	Grated Cheddar cheese	1/4 cup	60 mL
3.	Paprika, sprinkle		

- table fork
- microwave oven
- sharp knife
- cutting board
- table spoon
- small bowl
- measuring spoons
- dry measures
- microwave-safe plate
- microwave oven

1. Poke the potato several times with the fork. Microwave on high (100%) for 4 minutes, turning the potato over after 2 minutes. Let it stand for 2 minutes. Using the knife, cut the potato in half, lengthwise, on the cutting board. Using the spoon, scoop out the potato pulp from the centers, leaving the skins about 1/4 inch (6 mm) thick.

2. Mash the potato pulp well in the bowl with the fork. Add the margarine, onion salt, pepper, Parmesan cheese and sour cream. Stuff each potato shell with 1/2 of the mashed mixture. Place on the plate. Sprinkle with the Cheddar cheese.

3. Sprinkle each stuffed potato with paprika. Microwave on high (100%) for 2 minutes until hot and cheese is melted. Makes 2 potato boats.

Peanutty Pasta Sauce

Serve over pasta or, for a change, steamed vegetables. Also makes a good dipping sauce for chicken nuggets.

- measuring spoons
- frying pan
- mixing spoon
- dry measures
- liquid measures
- whisk
- small cup

1.	Cooking oil	2 tsp.	10 mL
	Small onion, chopped	1	1
	Garlic powder	1¼ tsp.	6 mL
2.	Peanut butter	½ cup	125 mL
	Apple juice	3 tbsp.	50 mL
	Soy sauce	1½ tbsp.	25 mL
	Ground ginger	1 tsp.	5 mL
	Pepper	¼ tsp.	1 mL
	Water	1½ cups	375 mL
3.	Evaporated milk	¼ cup	60 mL
	Cornstarch	2 tsp.	10 mL

1. Heat the cooking oil in the frying pan over medium heat. Sauté the onion in the oil for 2 minutes. Sprinkle with the garlic powder. Sauté for 1 minute.

2. Stir in the peanut butter and apple juice until smooth. Whisk in the soy sauce, ginger, pepper and water. Bring to a boil.

3. Combine the milk and cornstarch in the cup. Slowly stir into the boiling sauce. Cook for 2 minutes until thickened. If not using immediately, store, covered, in the refrigerator. Makes 2⅔ cups (650 mL).

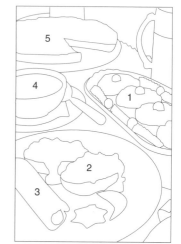

1. Ham Stacks, page 68
2. Broccoli-Sauced Potatoes, page 65
3. Corn Doggies, page 134
4. Bean 'N' Bacon Soup, page 129
5. Pass-Da Pizza, page 86

Loaded Quesadilla `hot`

Pronounced keh-sah-DEE-yah. This recipe can be increased to make as many quesadillas as you want.

1.
White (or whole wheat) flour tortilla (10 inch, 25 cm, size)	1	1
Salsa	2 tbsp.	30 mL
Grated Cheddar (or Monterey Jack) cheese (or a mixture of both)	1/3 cup	75 mL
Bacon slice, cooked crisp and crumbled	1	1
Finely chopped fresh vegetables (such as broccoli, green peppers, green onion or jalapeño peppers)	6 tbsp.	100 mL

- baking sheet with sides
- measuring spoons
- table knife
- dry measures
- oven mitts
- wire rack
- sharp knife

1. Place the oven rack in the center position. Turn the oven on to 400°F (205°C). Lay the tortilla flat on the baking sheet. Spread the salsa over one half of the tortilla. Sprinkle the cheese, bacon and vegetables over the salsa. Fold the plain half of the tortilla over the topped side. Bake for 5 to 8 minutes until the cheese is melted and the edges are crispy. Use the oven mitts to remove the baking sheet to the wire rack. Cut into wedges to eat. Makes 1 quesadilla.

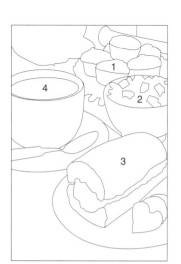

1. Gingerbran Cream Muffins, page 26
2. Cucumber & Pea Salad, page 92
3. Super Sausage Sub, page 110
4. Corn Chowder, page 128

Hot Lunches 73

- frying pan
- mixing spoon
- dry measures
- liquid measures
- measuring spoons
- small bowl

Sausage & Apple Bake

Cut the sausage with a wet knife to help avoid the build-up of meat. Wash the knife off if it does.

1.	**Pork (or pork and beef) sausages, cut crosswise into ¹/₂ inch (12 mm) rounds**	**1 lb.**	**454 g**
	Large apple, cored and diced	**1**	**1**
	Diced onion	**¹/₄ cup**	**60 mL**
2.	**Apple juice**	**2 cups**	**500 mL**
	Brown sugar, packed	**¹/₄ cup**	**60 mL**
	Ground cinnamon	**¹/₈ tsp.**	**0.5 mL**
	Cornstarch	**2¹/₂ tbsp.**	**37 mL**

1. Scramble-fry the sausage in the frying pan over medium heat for 2 minutes. Add the apple and onion. Stir and cook until onion is soft and the mixture is starting to brown.

2. Pour in the apple juice. Combine the remaining 3 ingredients in the bowl. Stir into the apple juice mixture. Bring to a boil to thicken slightly. Makes 5 cups (1.25 L).

Variation: Omit the cinnamon and use ¹/₄ tsp. (1 mL) of maple flavoring.

- dry measures
- small bowl
- table fork
- measuring spoons
- table knife
- baking sheet
- oven mitts
- wire rack

Pineapple Cheese Waffles (hot)

A boost in flavor to ordinary frozen waffles.

1.	**Creamed cottage cheese**	**¹/₂ cup**	**125 mL**
2.	**Brown sugar, packed**	**2 tsp.**	**10 mL**
	Ground cinnamon	**¹/₈ tsp.**	**0.5 mL**
	Frozen plain (or buttermilk) waffles	**2**	**2**
3.	**Canned pineapple slices, drained very well on paper towel**	**2**	**2**

Continued on the next page.

Hot Lunches

1. Place the oven rack in the center position. Turn the oven on to 350°F (175°C). Put the cottage cheese into the bowl. Mash with the fork until smooth and creamy.

2. Add the sugar and cinnamon. Spread the cheese mixture over the frozen waffles. Place on the ungreased baking sheet.

3. Lay the pineapple slices over the cheese mixture. Bake in the oven for 20 minutes until the cheese is hot and the waffle is crispy. Use the oven mitts to remove the baking sheet to the wire rack. Serve immediately. Makes 2 waffles.

Make-Ahead Cheese Toast chill hot

This is a great lunch for weekends. Surprise your family and make this for them. Prepare this the night before and simply pop in the oven the next day when ready to eat.

1.	White (or whole wheat) bread slices, crusts removed	8	8
	Cheddar cheese slices, to cover		
2.	Large eggs	2	2
	Prepared mustard	2 tsp.	10 mL
	Salt	¼ tsp.	1 mL
	Milk	½ cup	125 mL
	Paprika, sprinkle		

- 9 × 9 inch (22 × 22 cm) square baking pan
- bread knife
- measuring spoons
- small bowl
- table fork
- liquid measures
- plastic wrap
- oven mitts
- wire rack

1. Lightly grease the baking pan. Cover the bottom of the baking pan with 4 of the bread slices, trimming to fit. Top with the cheese. Cover with the remaining 4 bread slices, trimming to fit.

2. Beat the eggs, mustard and salt together in the bowl with the fork. Add the milk. Mix well. Pour evenly over the bread, making sure all the bread is covered. Sprinkle with paprika. Cover with plastic wrap and chill in the refrigerator for 2 hours or overnight. Place the oven rack in the center position. Turn the oven on to 350°F (175°C). Bake, uncovered, for 30 minutes. Use the oven mitts to remove the baking pan to the wire rack. Let stand for 2 or 3 minutes until set. Serves 4.

Mushroom Swiss Potato

A hearty stuffed potato that is quick to make (and nutritious).

- table fork
- paper towel
- microwave oven
- oven mitts
- cutting board
- measuring spoons
- frying pan
- mixing spoon
- sharp knife
- table spoon

1.	**Large potato, with peel**	**1**	**1**
2.	**Tub margarine**	**2 tsp.**	**10 mL**
	Large mushrooms, sliced	**4**	**4**
3.	**Garlic powder, sprinkle**		
	Pepper, sprinkle		
	Salt, sprinkle		
4.	**Process Swiss cheese slice,** **broken into pieces**	**1-2**	**1-2**

1. Poke the potato 3 or 4 times with the fork. Wrap in the paper towel and microwave on high (100%) for 7 minutes. Use the oven mitts to remove the potato to the cutting board to finish cooking.

2. Melt the margarine in the frying pan over medium heat. Add the mushrooms. Sauté for 1 minute.

3. Add the next 3 ingredients and sauté until the mushrooms are golden.

4. Cut a large X in the top of the potato, going in about 1 inch (2.5 cm). Push the bottom sides inward to open the X slightly. Lay the pieces of cheese on the potato and spoon the mushrooms over the top. Microwave on high (100%) for 30 to 40 seconds to melt the cheese. Makes 1 large stuffed potato.

Pictured on page 126.

Did you know?

Cleaning the microwave oven is a snap. Simply put a glass of water in the microwave oven. Heat on high (100%) for 2½ to 3 minutes until boiling and steaming. Use oven mitts to remove the glass of water. Wipe the walls with a damp dish cloth, then clean and shine them with a tea towel.

Creamed Eggs On Toast

Prepare the sauce while the eggs are boiling.

1.	Large eggs	4	4
	Cold water		
2.	Tub margarine	2 tbsp.	30 mL
	All-purpose flour	¼ cup	60 mL
	Milk	2 cups	500 mL
3.	Onion powder	¼ tsp.	1 mL
	Dried chives	½ tsp.	2 mL
	Salt	½ tsp.	2 mL
	Pepper, sprinkle		
	Garlic powder, sprinkle		
4.	Whole wheat (or white) bread slices	4	4
	Tub margarine (optional)		

- small saucepan
- measuring spoons
- medium saucepan
- dry measures
- whisk
- liquid measures
- mixing spoon
- sharp knife (or egg slicer)
- cutting board
- toaster
- table knife

1. Place the eggs in the small saucepan and cover with cold water to about 1 inch (2.5 cm) higher than the eggs. Bring to a boil over high heat. Reduce the heat to medium. Simmer for 10 minutes. Remove the saucepan from the heat and pour out the water from the pan. Keep covering the eggs with cold water until they are cold. Lightly crack the shells and let the eggs sit in the water while the sauce is being made.

2. Melt the margarine in the medium saucepan over medium heat. Stir in the flour. Whisk in the milk slowly so you don't get any lumps. Bring the mixture to a boil until thickened.

3. Stir in the onion powder, chives, salt, pepper and garlic powder. Peel the eggs and chop them on the cutting board or break them up using the egg slicer in both directions. Stir into the cream sauce. Makes 2⅔ cups (650 mL).

4. Toast the bread. Spread each slice with margarine if desired. Pour about ⅔ cup (150 mL) of egg sauce over each piece of toast to serve. Serves 4.

- baking sheet
- measuring spoons
- table knife
- dry measures
- oven mitts
- wire rack

Garden Pitas (hot)

The color and taste of a garden of vegetables.

1.	Mashed salsa (or pizza sauce)	2 tbsp.	30 mL
	Pita bread (8 inch, 20 cm, size)	1	1
2.	Grated carrot	1 tbsp.	15 mL
	Finely chopped green or red pepper	1 tbsp.	15 mL
	Finely chopped green onion	1 tbsp.	15 mL
	Diced tomato	2 tbsp.	30 mL
	Grated mozzarella cheese	¼ cup	60 mL

1. Place the oven rack in the upper position. Turn the oven on to broil. Lay the pita bread on the ungreased baking sheet. Spread the salsa over the pita bread.

2. Sprinkle the remaining 5 ingredients over the salsa. Broil in the oven until the cheese is melted and the edges are crisp and browned. Use the oven mitts to remove the baking sheet to the wire rack. Cuts into 6 wedges.

When broiling, take extra care and caution when it comes to the cooking time stated in the recipe. Watch carefully because food cooks very fast when close to the heating element in the oven.

Pizza Thingies (hot)

These individual pizzas may be wrapped well and frozen then thawed before baking. Wonderfully convenient for a hot lunch at home or bake and freeze for your lunch bag. They will be defrosted by lunch, then just heat in microwave oven for 30 to 60 seconds.

1.	**Bacon, diced**	**1 lb.**	**454 g**
	Sliced fresh mushrooms	**2 cups**	**500 mL**
2.	**Ketchup**	**1 cup**	**250 mL**
	Green onions, sliced	**2**	**2**
	Worcestershire sauce	**2 tsp.**	**10 mL**
	Dried whole oregano	**½ tsp.**	**2 mL**
	Dry mustard	**½ tsp.**	**2 mL**
3.	**Process cheese spread**	**⅓ cup**	**75 mL**
	Hamburger (or any other type) of bun, split in half	**6**	**6**
	Grated mozzarella cheese	**⅔ cup**	**150 mL**

- frying pan
- stirring spoon
- dry measures
- hot pad
- measuring spoons
- table knife
- baking sheet
- oven mitts
- wire rack

1. Place the oven rack in the bottom position. Turn the oven on to 400°F (205°C). Cook the bacon in the frying pan over medium heat for 5 to 6 minutes until just starting to become crisp. Drain and discard most of the fat. Add the mushrooms and continue to stir until the mushrooms are soft, bacon is browned and liquid is evaporated. Remove from the heat to the hot pad.

2. Stir in the next 5 ingredients.

3. Spread the process cheese on each of the 12 bun halves. Top each with 2 tbsp. (30 mL) of the bacon mixture, spreading evenly. Cover the mixture with the cheese. Place on the ungreased baking sheet. Bake for 6 minutes until the cheese is bubbly. Use the oven mitts to remove the baking sheet to the wire rack. Makes 12 pizzas.

Pizza Pinwheels hot

Best served hot from the oven rather than reheating. Tangy and attractive.

- baking sheet
- dry measures
- liquid measures
- medium bowl
- mixing spoon
- rolling pin
- ruler
- measuring spoons
- medium bowl
- sharp knife
- oven mitts
- wire rack

1.			
	Biscuit mix	2¼ cups	560 mL
	Water	½ cup	125 mL
	Biscuit mix, as needed, to prevent sticking when rolling		

2.			
	Commercial pizza (or tomato) sauce	7½ oz.	213 mL
	Green onions, sliced	2	2
	Finely chopped green or red pepper	½ cup	125 mL
	Finely chopped pepperoni (or other cooked sausage type of meat)	½ cup	125 mL
	Grated mozzarella cheese	1 cup	250 mL
	Dried whole oregano	¼ tsp.	1 mL

1. Place the oven rack in the center position. Turn oven on to 400°F (205°C). Grease the baking sheet. Combine the biscuit mix and water in the medium bowl until it starts to form a ball. Turn the dough out onto the counter that has been lightly dusted with more biscuit mix. Gently knead the dough 20 times. Dust with biscuit mix and roll out to a 12 × 12 inch (30 × 30 cm) rectangle.

2. Combine the remaining 6 ingredients in the small bowl. Mix well. Spread over the dough, leaving about 1 inch (2.5 cm) all around the outside edge. Roll up the dough from 1 side to the other like a jelly roll. Pinch along the long edge of the roll to seal. Cut into twelve 1 inch (2.5 cm) thick slices. Place on the baking sheet. Bake in the oven for 12 minutes. Use the oven mitts to remove the baking sheet to the wire rack. Makes 12 little pizzas.

Pictured on page 54.

Pita Pizzas  hot

These pizzas can be assembled and frozen before baking. When those hunger pangs hit, pop the frozen pizza in the oven and broil for eight to nine minutes.

1.	Pita breads	2	2
	Commercial pizza sauce	3 tbsp.	50 mL
2.	Any combination of the following toppings: chopped fresh mushrooms, chopped green pepper, chopped tomato, chopped green onion, pineapple tidbits, cooked crumbled bacon, deli meat (such as ham and pepperoni), to make	²/₃ cup	150 mL
3.	Grated mozzarella cheese	¹/₂ cup	125 mL

* measuring spoons
* spreading knife
* dry measures
* baking sheet
* oven mitts
* wire rack

1. Place the oven rack in the center position. Turn the oven on to broil. Spread each pita with 1¹/₂ tbsp. (25 mL) of the sauce. Be sure to spread it right to the edges.

2. Sprinkle each pita with ¹/₂ of the toppings.

3. Sprinkle the toppings with the cheese. Lay the pitas on the ungreased baking sheet. Broil for 8 to 9 minutes until the cheese is melted and the edges are crispy. Use the oven mitts to remove the baking sheet to the wire rack. Makes 2 pita pizzas.

Pictured on page 89.

Did you know?

Be careful to prevent cutting your knuckles when grating cheese. Hold a large piece of cheese in one hand and the grater in the other hand. Press the cheese firmly into the holes on the grater as you move the cheese from top to bottom. Continue until you have the amount of cheese needed.

Individual Stuffed Pizzas (hot)

Golden semi-circles of pizza delights! Fresh bread flavor.
Try a different filling each noon hour.

- baking sheet
- 1-3 medium bowls
- dry measures
- measuring spoons
- large bowl
- mixing spoons
- liquid measures
- table fork
- tea towel
- small saucepan
- oven mitts
- wire rack

1. **PIZZA BASE**

All-purpose flour	2 cups	500 mL
Salt	¼ tsp.	1 mL
Grated Parmesan cheese	1 tbsp.	15 mL
Envelope instant dry yeast (measure 1½ tsp., 7 mL)	½ x ¼ oz.	½ x 8 g
Hot water	¾ cup	175 mL
Olive (or cooking) oil	1 tbsp.	15 mL

2. **CHEESY CHICKEN FILLING**

Chopped cooked chicken	1 cup	250 mL
Finely diced celery	¼ cup	60 mL
Green onion, sliced	1	1
Grated mozzarella cheese	¾ cup	175 mL
Dried sweet basil	¼ tsp.	1 mL
Garlic salt	¼ tsp.	1 mL

3. **PEPPERONI FILLING**

Diced pepperoni	⅔ cup	150 mL
Commercial pizza sauce	⅓ cup	75 mL
Finely diced green pepper	¼ cup	60 mL
Grated carrot	¼ cup	60 mL
Grated mozzarella cheese	¾ cup	175 mL

4. **VEGETABLE FILLING**

Tub margarine	1 tbsp.	15 mL
All-purpose flour	1 tbsp.	15 mL
Milk	½ cup	125 mL
Bite-size pieces of cooked vegetables	1½ cups	375 mL
Garlic salt	¼ tsp.	1 mL
Pepper, sprinkle		
Grated mozzarella (or Cheddar) cheese	⅔ cup	150 mL
Grated Parmesan cheese	1 tbsp.	15 mL

Continued on the next page.

1. **Pizza Base:** Place the oven rack in the center position. Turn the oven on to 400°F (205°C). Grease the baking sheet and I medium bowl. Stir the flour, salt, Parmesan cheese and yeast together in the large bowl. Add the water and oil. Stir into the dry mixture with the fork until most of the flour is mixed in. Turn the dough out onto the counter that has been lightly dusted with some flour. Using your hands, and sprinkling flour, as needed, to keep dough from sticking, knead the dough for about 3 minutes until smooth and stretchy. Place in the greased bowl. Cover with the tea towel and set aside for 45 minutes while filling is being made. When filling is ready, punch down and knead the dough to remove air pockets. Divide into 4 even portions. Roll into balls and press each ball out evenly on lightly greased counter into a 6 inch (15 cm) circle. Continue assembling by following the directions with I of the fillings of your choice below.

2. **Cheesy Chicken Filling:** Combine all 6 ingredients well in the medium bowl. Makes $1^2/_3$ cups (400 mL) filling. Place 6 tbsp. (100 mL) of the filling on each of the dough circles to I side of the center. Fold the side without the filling over top of the filling and pinch the edges together well to seal. Place on the baking sheet. Bake in the oven for 20 minutes. Use the oven mitts to remove the pan to the wire rack. Makes 4 pizzas.

3. **Pepperoni Filling:** Combine all 5 ingredients well in the medium bowl. Makes $1^1/_2$ cups (375 mL) filling. Place $^1/_3$ cup (75 mL) of the filling on each of the dough circles to I side of the center. Fold the side without the filling over top of the filling and pinch the edges together well to seal. Place on the baking sheet. Bake in the oven for 20 minutes. Use the oven mitts to remove the pan to the wire rack. Makes 4 pizzas.

Pictured on page 108.

4. **Vegetable Filling:** Combine the margarine and flour in the small saucepan over medium heat. Add the milk, stirring until thickened. Stir in the 5 remaining ingredients, stirring until the cheese is melted and well combined. Cool. Makes $1^1/_2$ cups (375 mL) filling. Place $^1/_3$ cup (75 mL) of the cooled filling on each of the dough circles to I side of the center. Fold the side without the filling over top of the filling and pinch the edges together well to seal. Place on the baking sheet. Bake in the oven for 20 minutes. Use the oven mitts to remove the pan to the wire rack. Makes 4 pizzas.

Pizza Sticks (hot)

Slightly crusty golden strips of bread. Specks of sausage throughout. Nippy taste.

- baking sheet
- dry measures
- measuring spoons
- large bowl
- mixing spoons
- liquid measures
- rolling pin
- ruler
- sharp knife
- tea towel
- small cup
- pastry brush
- oven mitts
- wire rack
- small saucepan

1. **STICKS**

All-purpose flour	2 cups	500 mL
Salt	½ tsp.	2 mL
Granulated sugar	¼ tsp.	1 mL
Dried sweet basil	½ tsp.	2 mL
Envelope instant dry yeast	1 x ¼ oz.	1 x 8 g
(1 scant tbsp., 15 mL)		
Olive (or cooking) oil	1½ tbsp.	25 mL
Hot water	1 cup	250 mL
All-purpose flour,	½ cup	125 mL
approximately		
Chopped pepperoni	⅔ cup	150 mL

2.

Hard margarine, melted	2 tbsp.	30 mL
Garlic powder	¼ tsp.	1 mL

3. **DIPPING SAUCE**

Tomato sauce	7½ oz.	213 mL
Garlic salt	¼ tsp.	1 mL
Onion powder	¼ tsp.	1 mL
Dried whole oregano	½ tsp.	2 mL
Ketchup	2 tbsp.	30 mL
Granulated sugar, just a pinch		

1. **Sticks:** Place the oven rack in the center position. Grease the baking sheet. Stir the first 5 ingredients together in the bowl. Pour in the olive oil and hot water and stir together until the flour is combined. Work in the second amount of flour until no longer sticky. Turn out onto lightly floured surface. Knead for about 5 minutes, adding more flour as needed and a bit of the chopped pepperoni as you do, until all the pepperoni is mixed into the dough. Invert the bowl over the dough. Let the dough rest for 10 minutes. Roll the dough out to about ½ inch (12 mm) thick. Using the knife, cut rows about 1 inch (2.5 cm) wide and then cut crosswise into 5 inch (12.5 cm) sticks. Lay each stick on the baking sheet, about 2 inches (5 cm) apart. Cover with the tea towel. Let rise in the oven, with the door closed and the oven light on, for 30 minutes. Remove the baking sheet from the oven. Turn the oven on to 375°F (190°C).

Continued on the next page.

2. Combine the melted margarine and garlic powder in the cup.
   Brush the sticks with the margarine mixture. Bake in the oven for
   20 minutes. Use the oven mitts to remove the baking sheet to the
   wire rack. Makes 18 to 20 sticks.

3. **Dipping Sauce:** Combine all 6 ingredients in the small saucepan.
   Bring mixture to a simmer over low heat. Simmer for 15 minutes,
   stirring occasionally. Use as a dip for the pizza sticks. Makes $^3/_4$ cup
   (175 mL).

Pictured on page 125.

Tortilla Pizzas (hot)

Wedges are easy to hold in your hands to eat.

1. **White (or whole wheat) flour** **tortillas (10 inch, 25 cm, size)**	**2**	**2**
Commercial pizza sauce	**$^1/_4$ cup**	**60 mL**
2. **Finely chopped green pepper**	**$^1/_4$ cup**	**60 mL**
Finely chopped mushrooms	**$^1/_4$ cup**	**60 mL**
Grated mozzarella cheese	**1 cup**	**250 mL**
Dried whole oregano	**1 tsp.**	**5 mL**

- baking sheet
- dry measures
- table spoon
- measuring spoons
- oven mitts
- wire rack
- sharp knife

1. Place the oven rack in the center position. Turn the oven on to 375°F
   (190°C). Lay the 2 tortillas on the ungreased baking sheet. Spread
   2 tbsp. (30 mL) of the pizza sauce on each of the tortillas, using the
   back of the spoon, spreading sauce almost to the edges.

2. Divide and sprinkle the green pepper, mushrooms, cheese and
   oregano evenly over one half of each of the tortillas. Fold side without
   the filling over top of the filling to make a half-moon shape. Bake in
   the oven for 15 minutes until crisp and golden. Use the oven mitts to
   remove the baking sheet to the wire rack. Let stand for 5 minutes.
   Cut into wedges to serve. Makes 2 individual pizzas.

Pass-Da Pizza hot

The pasta makes the crust of the pizza. Very delicious.

- deep-dish 12 inch (30 cm) pizza pan
- liquid measures
- measuring spoons
- medium saucepan
- mixing spoon
- colander
- table fork
- oven mitts
- wire rack

1.	Water	8 cups	2 L
	Salt	1 tsp.	5 mL
	Cooking oil (optional)	1 tsp.	5 mL
	Spaghettini (or vermicelli) pasta	6 oz.	170 g
2.	Large egg	1	1
	Milk	2 tbsp.	30 mL
3.	Spaghetti sauce (your favorite kind)	1½ cups	375 mL
	Sliced pepperoni (or other spicy) sausage	¾ cup	175 mL
	Grated mozzarella cheese	1½ cups	375 mL
	Thinly sliced green pepper (or onion or mushrooms), to cover (optional)		
	Grated Parmesan cheese (optional)	¼ cup	60 mL

1. Place the oven rack in the center position. Turn the oven on to 350°F (175°C). Grease the pizza pan. Combine the water, salt and cooking oil in the saucepan. Stir. Bring to a boil. Add the pasta. Boil, uncovered, for 6 to 8 minutes until just tender. Drain the pasta in the colander. Rinse with cold water. Drain.

2. In the same saucepan, beat the egg and milk together with the fork. Return the pasta to the saucepan. Mix well. Turn into the pizza pan. Spread evenly.

3. Spread the spaghetti sauce on top. Sprinkle with the pepperoni, mozzarella cheese and green pepper. Top with the Parmesan cheese. Bake in the oven for 30 minutes. Use the oven mitts to remove the pizza pan to the wire rack. Let stand for 5 minutes. Cuts into 10 wedges.

Pictured on page 71.

Tortellini Salad chill

A colorful and tasty salad.

1.	Water	6 cups	1.5 L
	Salt	1 tsp.	5 mL
	Fresh (or dried) cheese-filled tortellini	1 cup	250 mL
2.	Diced English cucumber, with peel	1/2 cup	125 mL
	Small tomato, diced	1	1
	Thinly sliced green onion	1/4 cup	60 mL
	Thinly slivered green or red pepper	1/2 cup	125 mL
	Salt	1/2 tsp.	2 mL
	Pepper	1/8 tsp.	0.5 mL

GET READY GET SET!

- liquid measures
- measuring spoons
- large saucepan
- dry measures
- colander
- medium bowl
- mixing spoon
- plastic wrap

1. Bring the water and salt to a boil in the saucepan. Add the tortellini and cook for about 10 minutes until tender but still firm. Drain in the colander. Rinse with cold water until cool. Drain well.

2. Combine the pasta with the remaining 6 ingredients in the bowl. Stir well. Cover with plastic wrap. Chill in the refrigerator for 30 minutes to blend the flavors. Makes 3 1/2 cups (875 mL).

Pictured on page 107.

Did you know?

To peel a hard boiled egg, tap it on the kitchen counter to crack the shell. Roll it between your hands to loosen the shell. Hold it under cold water as you peel it.

Potato Salad (chill)

Dill pickles add a great flavor to this creamy salad.

- sharp knife
- cutting board
- liquid measures
- measuring spoons
- small saucepan
- medium bowl
- mixing spoon
- dry measures
- small cup
- plastic wrap

1.	**Medium potatoes, peeled**	**2**	**2**
	Water	**2 cups**	**500 mL**
	Salt	**¼ tsp.**	**1 mL**
2.	**Large hard-boiled eggs, chopped**	**2**	**2**
	Celery rib, thinly sliced	**1**	**1**
	Small dill pickles, chopped and blotted dry with paper towel	**3**	**3**
3.	**Mayonnaise (or salad dressing)**	**¼ cup**	**60 mL**
	Italian (or other non-creamy) dressing	**2 tbsp.**	**30 mL**
	Salt, sprinkle (optional)		
	Pepper, sprinkle (optional)		

1. Cut each of the potatoes into 4 pieces on the cutting board. Place the potato, water and salt in the saucepan. Cover. Bring to a boil over medium heat. Boil for about 15 minutes until tender. Drain. Place in the bowl to cool.

2. Add the egg, celery and pickles to the potato. Stir well.

3. Combine the mayonnaise and Italian dressing in the cup. Stir into the potato mixture. Sprinkle with salt and pepper. Stir. Cover with plastic wrap. Chill in the refrigerator for at least 30 minutes. Makes 2¾ cups (675 mL).

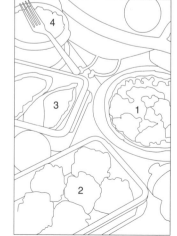

1. Pita Pizzas, page 81
2. Peanut Butter Popcorn Treats, page 121
3. Pickly Pita Pockets, page 101
4. Macaroni & Cottage Cheese, page 58

Salads

Marinated Vegetables chill

This salad will keep for one week in the refrigerator. The flavor just keeps getting better.

1.	Broccoli florets	2 cups	500 mL
	Cauliflower florets	2 cups	500 mL
	Water	1 tbsp.	15 mL
2.	Thinly sliced carrot	1 cup	250 mL
	Sliced celery	½ cup	125 mL
	Green onion, sliced	1	1
	Medium red or yellow pepper, sliced	1	1
	Diced English cucumber, with peel	1 cup	250 mL
3.	Italian (or other non-creamy) dressing	½ cup	125 mL

- dry measures
- medium microwave-safe bowl with lid (or plastic wrap)
- measuring spoons
- microwave oven
- oven mitts
- hot pad
- large bowl
- mixing spoon
- liquid measures

1. Combine the broccoli and cauliflower in the bowl. Sprinkle with the water. Cover the bowl, leaving a small opening for the steam to escape. Microwave on high (100%) for 2 minutes. Use the oven mitts to remove the bowl to the hot pad. Let stand, covered, for 2 minutes.

2. Place the next 5 ingredients in the large bowl. Add the broccoli and cauliflower. Stir.

3. Pour the dressing over the vegetables. Stir well. Chill in the refrigerator until cold. Makes 8 cups (2 L).

Pictured on the back cover.

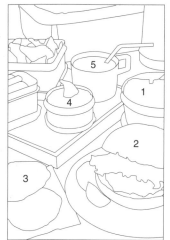

1. Crunchy Potato Salad, page 96
2. Tuna Buns, page 115
3. Easy Raisin Cookies, page 23
4. Hot Tortilla Dip, page 32
5. Veggie Cooler, page 14

Salads

91

- dry measures
- measuring spoons
- small bowl
- mixing spoon

Rice Salad

This salad can also be stuffed into a pita bread for a salad sandwich.

1.			
Cooked rice	¾ cup	175 mL
Cooked ham, chopped	2 oz.	56 g
Green onion, sliced	2 tbsp.	30 mL
Cooked vegetables (such as peas, broccoli florets or green beans)	½ cup	125 mL
Grated carrot	¼ cup	60 mL
Olive oil	1 tsp.	5 mL
White (or wine or cider) vinegar	2 tsp.	10 mL
Salt, sprinkle		

1. Combine all 8 ingredients in the bowl. Mix well. Makes 1½ cups (375 mL).

Pictured on page 126.

Variation: Add 2 tbsp. (30 mL) of sunflower seeds or pumpkin seeds, or add ¼ cup (60 mL) of raisins.

- dry measures
- measuring spoons
- small bowl
- mixing spoon
- small cup
- table spoon

Cucumber & Pea Salad

You can make this salad the night before to take to school the next day. A crunchy, refreshing salad.

1.			
Diced English cucumber, with peel	1 cup	250 mL
Frozen baby peas, thawed	½ cup	125 mL
Sliced green onion	2 tbsp.	30 mL
Garlic salt, sprinkle		
Pepper, sprinkle		
Cubed Cheddar (or Swiss) cheese (½ inch, 12 mm, size)	½ cup	125 mL

Continued on the next page.

2. DRESSING

Mayonnaise (or salad dressing)	2 tbsp.	30 mL
Granulated sugar	2 tsp.	10 mL
Lemon juice	1 tsp.	5 mL

1. Combine the first 6 ingredients in the bowl. Stir well.

2. Dressing: Mix the mayonnaise, sugar and lemon juice in the cup. Add to the vegetable mixture. Mix well. Makes 2 cups (500 mL).

Pictured on page 72.

Tomato & Mozza Salad

This salad tastes even better when left to stand awhile. Great to take for lunch.

1.	**Medium tomatoes**	2	2
2.	**Olive oil**	2 tsp.	10 mL
	Garlic salt	¼ tsp.	1 mL
	Pepper, sprinkle		
	Dried sweet basil	¼ tsp.	1 mL
	Sliced green onion	1 tbsp.	15 mL
	Black olives, sliced (optional)	4	4
3.	**Grated mozzarella cheese**	½ cup	125 mL

- sharp knife
- cutting board
- paper towel
- small bowl
- measuring spoons
- mixing spoon
- dry measures

1. Cut the tomato in half on the cutting board. Gently squeeze the tomato halves over the paper towel to remove the seeds. Discard the seeds and juice. Dice the tomato into bite-size pieces. Place in the bowl.

2. Add the next 6 ingredients. Stir.

3. Stir in the cheese. Makes 1½ cups (375 mL).

Pictured on page 36.

Variation: Spoon salad onto baguette slices. Place slices on a baking sheet. Broil on the top rack in the oven until the cheese is melted.

- medium bowl
- mixing spoon
- liquid measures
- small bowl
- whisk
- covered container

Lemon Sauced Fruit

Chunks of fruit in a colorful syrup. Can be a fruit salad or a dessert.

1.	**Canned fruit cocktail, drained, juice reserved**	**14 oz.**	**398 mL**
	Canned mandarin orange segments, drained, juice reserved	**10 oz.**	**284 mL**
	Medium bananas, diced	**2**	**2**
2.	**Reserved fruit cocktail and mandarin orange juice, plus pineapple, apple or orange juice, to make**	**1½ cups**	**375 mL**
	Instant lemon pudding powder, 4 serving size	**1**	**1**

1. Combine the fruit cocktail, oranges and banana in the medium bowl. Stir.

2. Combine the reserved juices and pudding powder in the small bowl. Whisk for 2 minutes. Fold into the fruit. Store any remaining salad in the container in the refrigerator for up to 5 days. Makes 4 cups (1 L).

Bean & Tomato Salad (chill)

A delicious crunchy salad. Perfect to take to school for lunch.

1.	**Canned chick peas (garbanzo beans), drained and rinsed**	**19 oz.**	**540 mL**
	Thinly sliced celery	**½ cup**	**125 mL**
	Green onion, thinly sliced	**1**	**1**
	Diced red pepper	**½ cup**	**125 mL**
	Canned stewed tomatoes, drained and chopped	**14 oz.**	**398 mL**

Continued on the next page.

- dry measures
- medium bowl
- mixing spoon
- measuring spoons
- small bowl
- plastic wrap
- covered container

94 **Salads**

2. DRESSING

Olive (or vegetable) oil	2 tbsp.	30 mL
White vinegar	2 tbsp.	30 mL
Dried sweet basil	1/2 tsp.	2 mL
Dry mustard	1/4 tsp.	1 mL
Garlic powder	1/8 tsp.	0.5 mL
Parsley flakes	2 tsp.	10 mL

1. Combine the first 5 ingredients in the medium bowl. Stir well.

2. **Dressing:** Combine the remaining 6 ingredients in the small bowl. Pour over the vegetable mixture. Mix well. Cover with plastic wrap. Marinate in the refrigerator for several hours or overnight, stirring several times. Store any remaining salad in the container in the refrigerator for up to 3 days. Makes 4 cups (1 L).

Pictured on page 53.

Cottage Cheese Salad

Very colorful. A great blend of flavors.

1. Creamed cottage cheese	1 cup	250 mL
Diced English cucumber, with peel	1/4 cup	60 mL
Grated carrot	2 tbsp.	30 mL
Diced red pepper	2 tbsp.	30 mL
Garlic salt	1/8 tsp.	0.5 mL
Pepper, sprinkle		
Celery seed, sprinkle		

1. Combine all 7 ingredients in the bowl. Stir. Let the salad stand for 10 minutes to blend the flavors. Store any remaining salad in the container in the refrigerator for up to 24 hours. Makes 1 1/2 cups (375 mL).

Pictured on page 17.

- dry measures
- measuring spoons
- small bowl
- mixing spoon
- covered container

- sharp knife
- cutting board
- liquid measures
- measuring spoons
- small saucepan
- colander
- medium bowl
- mixing spoon
- plastic wrap

Crunchy Potato Salad chill

Very colorful. Watch the cooking time of the potato. It will differ according to the size of your potato.

1.	Large potato, peeled	1	1
	Water	1 cup	250 mL
	Salt	¼ tsp.	1 mL
2.	Diced red pepper	2 tbsp.	30 mL
	Grated carrot	1 tbsp.	15 mL
	Finely diced celery	1 tbsp.	15 mL
	Sliced green onion	1 tbsp.	15 mL
	Grated Cheddar cheese	2 tbsp.	30 mL
	Italian dressing	2 tbsp.	30 mL
	Salt, sprinkle		
	Pepper, sprinkle		

1. Cut the potato crosswise into 3 pieces on the cutting board. Put the potato pieces, water and salt into the saucepan. Bring to a boil. Reduce the heat to low. Cover. Simmer for about 13 minutes until the potato is tender when poked with the knife. Do not overcook or else the potato will be mushy. Drain in the colander. Cool slightly. Dice into small cubes on the cutting board.

2. Combine the potato and the remaining 8 ingredients in the bowl. Stir. Cover with plastic wrap. Chill in the refrigerator until cold. Makes 1½ cups (375 mL).

Pictured on page 90.

Did you know?

You can use a thermos to bring your salad for lunch. Chill a wide-mouth thermos with ice water and let stand for 5 minutes. Drain thermos and fill with thoroughly chilled salad.

Peas 'N' Pasta Salad

Best eaten the same day. If you would like to save half of this salad to take in your lunch tomorrow, simply pour 3 tbsp. (50 mL) of the dressing now, and save 3 tbsp. (50 mL) to pour over the salad before you go to school.

1.	Water	6 cups	1.5 L
	Salt	1 tsp.	5 mL
	Cooking oil (optional)	1 tsp.	5 mL
	Fusilli (or rotini) pasta	1 cup	250 mL
	Frozen baby peas	½ cup	125 mL
2.	Sliced green onion	2 tbsp.	30 mL
	Grated carrot	2 tbsp.	30 mL
	Small tomato	1	1
	Cubed Cheddar (or other firm) cheese, (½ inch, 12 mm, size)	½ cup	125 mL
	Italian (or other non-creamy) dressing	⅓ cup	75 mL

- liquid measures
- large saucepan
- measuring spoons
- dry measures
- mixing spoon
- colander
- medium bowl
- sharp knife
- cutting board
- paper towel
- liquid measures

1. Bring the water in the saucepan to a boil over high heat. Add the salt and cooking oil. Add the fusilli. When the water returns to a boil, reduce the heat to medium-high. Cook the pasta for 8 minutes, stirring occasionally. Add the peas to the pasta and water. Cook for 1 minute until the pasta is tender but still firm. Drain in the colander. Run cold water over. Drain well.

2. Combine the green onion and carrot in the bowl. Add the pasta and peas. Cut the tomato in half on the cutting board. Gently squeeze the tomato halves over the paper towel to remove the seeds. Discard the seeds and juice. Dice the tomato into ½ inch (12 mm) chunks. Add to the bowl. Add the cheese. Stir in the dressing just before serving. Makes 3½ cups (875 mL).

Pictured on the front cover.

- frying pan
- tongs
- paper towel
- measuring spoons
- table knife

Peanut Butter & Bacon Sandwich

Make this sandwich and wrap it with plastic wrap and take it to school. Heat in the microwave oven when ready for lunch.

1.	Bacon slices (see Note)	2	2
2.	Peanut butter	1½ tbsp.	25 mL
	White (or whole wheat) bread slices, toasted	2	2
	Process Mozzarella cheese slice	1	1
	Tub margarine	1½ tsp.	7 mL

1. Cook the bacon in the frying pan over medium heat until crisp. Use the tongs to turn the bacon. Remove the bacon to the paper towel, blotting well.

2. Spread the peanut butter on 1 slice of toast. Break each slice of bacon into 2 pieces. Lay all 4 pieces over the peanut butter. Top with the cheese slice. Spread the other slice of toast with the margarine. Place, buttered side down, over the cheese. Makes 1 sandwich.

Note: Bacon may be cooked in the microwave oven instead of a frying pan. Simply place the bacon between paper towels and microwave on high (100%) for 3 minutes until crisp. Remove to a clean paper towel and blot well to remove the fat.

Ham & Cuke Sandwich

Yummy to eat for lunch any day of the week.

1. | | | |
    |---|---|---|
    | Mayonnaise (or salad dressing) | 2 tsp. | 10 mL |
    | French (or Russian) dressing | 2 tsp. | 10 mL |
    | Whole wheat (or white) bread slices | 2 | 2 |

2. | | | |
    |---|---|---|
    | Shaved ham slices (about 2 oz., 56 g) | 2 | 2 |
    | English cucumber slices, with peel | 3-4 | 3-4 |

1. Combine the mayonnaise and French dressing in the bowl. Mix well. Spread mixture on both slices of bread.

2. Place the ham slices on 1 slice of bread. Top with the cucumber slices. Place the second slice of bread on top. Cut in half on the cutting board. Makes 1 sandwich.

Pictured on page 36.

- measuring spoons
- small bowl
- mixing spoon
- table knife
- bread knife
- cutting board

Sandwiches made from frozen bread and wrapped immediately in plastic wrap will keep the filling fresh and crisp for hours.

- measuring spoons
- table knife
- dry measures

Sliced Turkey Pita

The perfect lunch when you have leftover turkey.

1.			
Plain spreadable cream cheese	3 tbsp.	50 mL
Pita bread (4½-5 inch, 11.5-12.5 cm, size), cut in half	1	1
Cranberry sauce	2 tbsp.	30 mL
Turkey slices	4	4
Alfalfa sprouts (or shredded lettuce)	½ cup	125 mL

1. Spread the cream cheese on the inner top side of each pita half. Spread the cranberry sauce on the inner bottom side of each pocket. Place 1 slice of turkey in each pocket. Top each slice with the sprouts. Place second slice of turkey over the sprouts. Makes 2 filled pita halves.

- toaster
- measuring spoons
- table knife
- bread knife
- cutting board

Veggie Bagel

A messy, but delicious stacked sandwich that's ready in minutes!

1. Whole wheat (or multi-grain) bagel, cut in half	1	1
2. Plain (or herbed) spreadable cream cheese	1 tbsp.	15 mL
English cucumber slices, with peel	3-4	3-4
Tomato slices	1-2	1-2
3. Salt, sprinkle		
Pepper, sprinkle		
Alfalfa sprouts (optional)	1-2 tbsp.	15-30 mL

Continued on the next page.

Sandwiches

1. Toast the bagel halves until lightly browned.

2. Spread the cream cheese on both halves. Lay the cucumber and tomato slices on top on 1 half.

3. Sprinkle with salt and pepper. Add the alfalfa sprouts. Top with the second half of the bagel. Cut in half on the cutting board. Makes 1 bagel.

Pickly Pita Pockets

A delicious crunch to it. Eat now or make ahead and cover and refrigerate overnight.

1.			
Diced ham (or beef roast or salami)	1 cup	250 mL	
Finely chopped dill pickles, blotted dry with paper towel	⅓ cup	75 mL	
Mayonnaise (or salad dressing)	2 tbsp.	30 mL	
Prepared mustard	1 tsp.	5 mL	
Pita breads (4½-5 inch, 11.5-12.5 cm, size), cut in half	2	2	

- dry measures
- measuring spoons
- small bowl
- mixing spoon

1. Combine the ham, pickles, mayonnaise and mustard in the bowl. Mix well. Fill each pita half with ⅓ cup (75 mL) of the filling. Makes 4 pita halves.

Pictured on page 89.

If you are taking a juice box in your lunch, freeze it overnight and pack it in your lunch in the morning. It will keep sandwiches cold and will be thawed by lunchtime.

The "New" Peanut Butter Sandwich

Alfalfa sprouts give peanut butter sandwiches a new kick! Great to wash down with a big glass of milk.

- measuring spoons
- table knife
- dry measures
- bread knife
- cutting board

1.	Peanut butter	2 tbsp.	30 mL
	White (or whole wheat) bagel, cut in half (toasted or fresh)	1	1
	Jam (your favorite flavor)	2 tsp.	10 mL
	Liquid honey	1 tsp.	5 mL
	Packed alfalfa sprouts	¹/₂ cup	125 mL

1. Spread the peanut butter on each bagel half. Spread 1 of the bagel halves with jam and honey. Top with the sprouts. Press both bagel halves together. Cut in half on the cutting board. Makes 1 sandwich.

Hero Sandwich

You will be a hero if you can finish this! You will be an even bigger hero if you share!

- bread knife
- cutting board
- measuring spoons
- table knife

1.	Submarine buns (12 inches, 30 cm, long)	1	1
	Mayonnaise (or salad dressing)	1 tbsp.	15 mL
	Prepared mustard	2 tsp.	10 mL
2.	Thin slices of salami (about 1¹/₂ oz., 42 g)	6	6
	Thinly shaved deli ham (or chicken or turkey)	1¹/₂ oz.	42 g
	Tomato slices	5	5
	Mozzarella (or Monterey Jack) cheese, thinly sliced	2 oz.	56 g
	Shredded lettuce (or mixed sprouts)	¹/₂ cup	125 mL
	Salt, sprinkle		
	Pepper, sprinkle		

Continued on the next page.

1. Cut the submarine bun in half horizontally on the cutting board. Pull out bits of bread from the soft center of the top and bottom halves, making a shallow hollow. Spread the mayonnaise on each half. Spread the mustard on the bottom half.

2. Layer the next 4 ingredients on top of the mustard-topped half. Top with the lettuce. Sprinkle with salt and pepper. Place the top half onto the filled bottom half. Press down slightly. Cut in half on the cutting board. Makes 1 sandwich.

Pictured on the front cover.

Muffuletta

Pronounced muhf-ful-LEHT-tuh. Make this New Orleans sandwich the night before to take for lunch the next day.

1. Italian-style crusty bun, cut in half horizontally	1	1
Italian dressing	1½ tbsp.	25 mL
Tomato slices	4	4
Mozzarella cheese slices	2	2
Lean ham (or beef) slices (about 2 oz., 56 g)	2	2
Alfalfa sprouts (or shredded lettuce)	⅓ cup	75 mL

- measuring spoons
- small cup
- pastry brush
- dry measures

1. Pull out bits of bread from the soft center of both bun halves. Put the dressing into the cup. Use the pastry brush to spread about ½ tbsp. (7 mL) of dressing on each half. Layer 2 slices of tomatoes, 1 slice of cheese and 1 slice of ham on the bottom half of the bun. Brush the remaining dressing over the ham. Top with the sprouts, remaining cheese slice and remaining tomato slices. Cover with the top half of the bun. Press the sandwich lightly together. Makes 1 sandwich.

- dry measures
- table knife
- muffin pan (for 12 muffins)
- oven mitts
- wire rack

Toast Cups  hot

Fill these with any sandwich filling.

| 1. | White (or whole wheat) bread slices, crusts removed | 12 | 12 |
| | Tub margarine | ⅓ cup | 75 mL |

1. Place the oven rack in the center position. Turn the oven on to 350°F (175°C). Thinly spread 1 side of each bread slice with the margarine. Press each slice, buttered side down, into each ungreased muffin cup. Bake in the oven for 15 to 20 minutes until crisp and toasted. Use the oven mitts to remove the muffin pan to the wire rack to cool. Makes 12 toast cups.

GARLIC TOAST CUPS: Stir ¼ tsp. (1 mL) of garlic powder into the margarine before spreading onto the bread slices.

- dry measures
- measuring spoons
- small bowl
- mixing spoon

Crunchy Egg Filling

Try using a pastry blender to chop up the hard-boiled eggs. It works very well. A great filling for sandwiches or Toast Cups, above.

1.	Large hard-boiled eggs, peeled and chopped	3	3
	Finely chopped cucumber, with peel	½ cup	125 mL
	Grated carrot	2 tbsp.	30 mL
	Thousand Island (or your favorite creamy) dressing	1½-2 tbsp.	25-30 mL
	Salt, sprinkle		
	Pepper, sprinkle		

1. Combine all 6 ingredients in the bowl. Mix well. Makes 1⅓ cups (325 mL).

Bacon & Egg Filler

If you like bacon and eggs, have your breakfast for lunch.

1.	Large hard-boiled egg, peeled and chopped	1	1
	Bacon slice, cooked crisp and crumbled (or 1 tsp., 5 mL, simulated bacon bits)	1	1
	Finely chopped green onion (optional)	2 tsp.	10 mL
	Mayonnaise (or salad dressing)	1 tbsp.	15 mL
	Salt, sprinkle		
	Pepper, sprinkle		
2.	Toast Cups, page 104	2	2

- measuring spoons
- small bowl
- mixing spoon

1. Combine the first 6 ingredients in the bowl. Stir until moistened.

2. Fill the Toast Cups. Makes ⅓ cup (75 mL).

Cream Cheese & Grape Jelly Sandwiches

This is very quick and easy to make for lunch.

1.	Spreadable cream cheese	2 tbsp.	30 mL
	White (or whole wheat) bread slices	2	2
	Grape jelly	4 tsp.	20 mL

- measuring spoons
- table knife
- bread knife
- cutting board

1. Spread the cream cheese on each slice of bread. Spread the jelly on top of the cream cheese on 1 of the slices. Top with the second slice of bread. Cut in half on the cutting board. Makes 1 sandwich.

GET READY GET SET!

- bread knife
- cutting board
- measuring spoons
- pastry brush
- dry measures

Pepper Cheese Roll

Colored peppers make this a real treat. This can be made ahead and wrapped with plastic wrap and refrigerated for up to two days.

1.			
Whole wheat roll, oblong (or oval) shape (about 5 inches, 12.5 cm, long)	1	1
Italian dressing	1 tbsp.	15 mL
Red, orange or yellow pepper, cut into thin strips	½	½
Pepper, sprinkle		
Dried sweet basil, just a pinch		
White cheese (such as mozzarella, Swiss or Monterey Jack), thinly sliced	2 oz.	56 g
Alfalfa (or mixed) sprouts (optional)	¼ cup	60 mL

1. Cut the roll in half horizontally on the cutting board. Remove a bit of bread from the soft center of the top and bottom halves, making a slight hollow. Brush the dressing onto each half of the roll. Layer the pepper strips lengthwise across the bottom half. Sprinkle with pepper and basil. Lay the cheese slices over top. Cover with the sprouts. Lay the top half of the roll over the sprouts. Makes 1 sandwich.

Pictured on page 17.

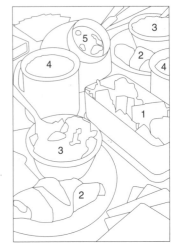

1. Ham & Melon Kabobs, page 40
2. Ham & Cheese Delights, page 133
3. Tortellini Salad, page 87
4. Eggnog, page 14
5. Fruity Granola, page 118

Sandwiches

Peanut Butter & Pickle Sandwich

Who would have thought! Sounds interesting—but very tasty!

1.	Peanut butter	2 tbsp.	30 mL
	White (or whole wheat) bread slices	2	2
2.	Dill pickles, cut in half lengthwise	1-2	1-2

- measuring spoons
- table knife
- paper towel
- bread knife
- cutting board

1. Spread the peanut butter on 1 side of each bread slice.

2. Lay the pickle on the paper towel for 1 to 2 minutes to soak up the juice. Lay the pickle slices on top of the peanut butter. Place second slice of bread on top, peanut butter side down. Cut in half on the cutting board. Makes 1 sandwich.

Variation: Spread peanut butter on a flour tortilla. Lay a small whole dill pickle on top of the tortilla at 1 end. Roll the tortilla around the pickle.

Pictured on page 36.

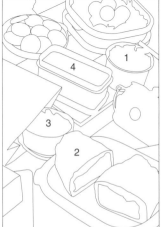

1. Citrus Crunchies, page 118
2. Individual Stuffed Pizzas, page 82
3. Toasted Pumpkin Seeds, page 119
4. Peanut Butter Pudding Dip, page 31

Sandwiches 109

Super Sausage Sub

These will freeze well. Simply thaw before heating or pop in your lunch bag in the morning and by noon, the sub is well thawed. Heat in the microwave for one minute. A great lunch!

- non-stick frying pan
- mixing spoon
- measuring spoons
- liquid measures
- dry measures

1.			
	Ground sausage meat	1 lb.	454 g
	Medium green pepper, cut into slivers	1	1
	Medium onion, sliced	1	1
	Pepper	¹⁄₈ tsp.	0.5 mL
	Paprika	¹⁄₂ tsp.	2 mL
	Cayenne pepper, sprinkle		
	Commercial meatless spaghetti sauce	1 cup	250 mL
2.			
	Submarine buns (10 inches, 25 cm, long), cut in half horizontally	4	4
	Grated Cheddar (or mozzarella) cheese	1 cup	250 mL

1. Scramble-fry the sausage in the frying pan over medium heat for 10 minutes, breaking up any large lumps as it cooks. Drain. Add the green pepper, onion, pepper, paprika and cayenne pepper. Scramble-fry for 10 minutes until the vegetables are tender-crisp and the sausage is no longer pink. Stir in the spaghetti sauce. Remove from the heat. Makes 3 cups (750 mL).

2. Pull out bits of bread from the soft center of the top and bottom halves of the buns, making a shallow hollow. Divide the sausage mixture among the 4 bottom bun halves. Top each with ¹⁄₄ cup (60 mL) of the cheese. Lay the top bun halves over the filling to make a sandwich. Ready to eat. Makes 4 sandwiches.

Pictured on page 72.

Variation: These can be heated in the microwave oven on medium (50%) for 1 minute or wrapped with foil and heated in a 300°F (150°C) oven for 15 minutes.

Barbecue Beef Buns hot

Great warm or cold. These freeze well. Simply take from the freezer and put it in your lunch bag. At lunchtime, warm in the microwave on high (100%) for one minute.

1.	**Lean ground beef**	**¹/₂ lb.**	**225 g**
	Small onion, cut into rings	**1**	**1**
2.	**Seasoning salt**	**¹/₂ tsp.**	**2 mL**
	Paprika	**¹/₂ tsp.**	**2 mL**
	Regular (or smoky-flavored) barbecue sauce	**¹/₂ cup**	**125 mL**
3.	**Refrigerator crescent-style rolls (tube of 8)**	**8 oz.**	**235 g**

- non-stick frying pan
- mixing spoon
- measuring spoons
- liquid measures
- baking sheet
- oven mitts
- wire rack

1. Place the oven rack in the center position. Turn the oven on to 375°F (190°C). Scramble-fry the ground beef in the frying pan over medium heat until almost brown. Add the onion rings. Scramble-fry for 2 minutes until the ground beef is no longer pink and the onion is soft.

2. Stir in the salt and paprika. Add the barbecue sauce. Simmer, uncovered, for 10 minutes until the liquid is gone. Cool.

3. Open the crescent rolls and separate into 8 triangles. Place 2 tbsp. (30 mL) of the beef mixture on each triangle. Bring the 3 points of each triangle to the center over the meat and pinch all of the edges together well to seal. Form into round shapes. Place each ball, seam side down on the ungreased baking sheet. Bake in the oven for 12 to 15 minutes until golden. Use the oven mitts to remove the baking sheet to the wire rack. Makes 8 buns.

Did you know?

Cook food in the microwave oven for the minimum time stated in the recipe. If more cooking time is required, add only 30 seconds at a time. It's better to add more time and cook the food just right rather than overcook the food.

- dry measures
- measuring spoons
- medium bowl
- mixing spoon
- broiler pan
- oven mitts
- wire rack
- pancake lifter

Apple Burgers (hot)

Try topping the patty with applesauce instead of mustard and ketchup.

1.			
Lean ground chicken (or turkey)	1 lb.	454 g
Applesauce, page 20	½ cup	125 mL
Finely chopped onion	2 tbsp.	30 mL
Finely chopped green or red pepper	2 tbsp.	30 mL
Seasoning salt	¾ tsp.	4 mL
Pepper	⅛ tsp.	0.5 mL
2. Hamburger buns, split in half (fresh or toasted)	6	6

1. Place the oven rack in the top position. Turn the oven on to broil. Mix all 6 ingredients in the bowl. Divide the mixture into 6 portions. Form each portion into a patty. Place on the ungreased broiler pan. Broil in the oven for 8 minutes. Use the oven mitts to remove the broiler pan to the wire rack. Flip the patties over with the pancake lifter. Bake for 8 minutes until patties are lightly browned and no longer pink inside.

2. Place 1 patty on the bottom half of each bun. Cover with the top halves of the buns. Makes 6 burgers.

When using a liquid measure, place it on a level counter. Bend down and watch as you fill it. Fill only to the line marking the amount called for in the recipe. Liquid measures shouldn't be used for ingredients such as flour or margarine because they cannot be leveled accurately.

Tuna Biscuits (hot)

Very tasty. Great to take for lunch instead of a sandwich.

1.	Large eggs, fork-beaten	2	2
	Mayonnaise (or salad dressing)	1/4 cup	60 mL
	Tub margarine, melted	2 tbsp.	30 mL
	Lemon juice	1/2 tbsp.	7 mL
	Hot pepper sauce	1/8 tsp.	0.5 mL
2.	Cheese-flavored crackers, coarsely crushed	22	22
	Canned solid tuna, drained and flaked	6.5 oz.	184 g
	Green onion, sliced	1	1
	Finely diced green pepper (optional)	2 tbsp.	30 mL

- muffin pan (for 8 large or 16 mini muffins)
- dry measures
- measuring spoons
- medium bowl
- whisk
- mixing spoon
- oven mitts
- wire rack

1. Place the oven rack in the center position. Turn the oven on to 375°F (190°C). Grease 8 large cups, or 16 mini cups, in the muffin pan. Combine the eggs, mayonnaise, margarine, lemon juice and pepper sauce in the bowl. Beat with the whisk until well blended.

2. Stir the cracker crumbs into the egg mixture. Add the tuna, green onion and pepper. Stir well to combine. Fill the muffin cups with the mixture. Bake in the oven for 20 minutes for the large cups or for 15 minutes for the mini cups. Use the oven mitts to remove the pan to the wire rack. Makes 8 large biscuits or 16 mini biscuits.

Did you know?

Instead of rushing to make your lunch in the morning before school, try doing as much as possible the night before . . . who knows, you may even have more time to sleep in!

Chick 'N' Cheese Burgers

Burgers may be made ahead and frozen individually. Simply place frozen burger in your lunch bag in the morning and microwave on high (100%) for one minute to heat at lunchtime.

- measuring spoons
- frying pan
- mixing spoon
- liquid measures
- dry measures

1.	Cooking oil	1 tsp.	5 mL
	Lean ground chicken	1 lb.	454 g
	Medium onion, chopped	1	1
	Celery rib, chopped	1	1
2.	All-purpose flour	3 tbsp.	50 mL
	Salt	½ tsp.	2 mL
	Pepper	¼ tsp.	1 mL
	Garlic powder, just a pinch (optional)		
	Milk	¾ cup	175 mL
3.	Grated Cheddar cheese	1½ cups	375 mL
	Process Cheddar cheese slices, broken up	2	2
	Prepared mustard	2 tsp.	10 mL
4.	Hamburger buns, cut in half	6	6

1. Heat the cooking oil in the frying pan over medium heat. Scramble-fry the chicken, onion and celery in the oil until the chicken is no longer pink and the vegetables are tender-crisp.

2. Sprinkle with the flour, salt, pepper and garlic powder. Stir for 1 minute. Stir in the milk gradually until bubbling and thickened.

3. Add the next 3 ingredients. Stir until the cheese is melted. Makes 3⅓ cups (825 mL).

4. Pull out bits of bread from the soft center of the top and bottom halves of the buns, making a shallow hollow. Fill each of the 6 bottom halves with a heaping ½ cup (125 mL) of the chicken mixture. Cover with the top halves of the buns. Makes 6 burgers.

Tuna Buns

Great warm or cold.

1.	**Canned flaked tuna in water, with liquid**	6½ oz.	184 g
	Large egg, fork-beaten	1	1
	Minced onion flakes	1 tsp.	5 mL
	Small carrot, grated	1	1
	Fine dry bread crumbs	½ cup	125 mL
	Parsley flakes	1 tsp.	5 mL
	Lemon juice	1 tsp.	5 mL
	Salt, sprinkle		
	Pepper, sprinkle		
2.	**Cooking oil**	1 tsp.	5 mL
3.	**Mayonnaise (or salad dressing)**	2 tbsp.	30 mL
	Kaiser buns, split	4	4
	Lettuce leaves	4	4

- measuring spoons
- dry measures
- medium bowl
- mixing spoon
- frying pan
- pancake lifter
- table knife

1. Combine the first 9 ingredients in the bowl. Mix well. Form into 4 patties.

2. Heat the cooking oil in the frying pan over medium heat. Cook the patties for about 2 minutes until golden brown. Turn the patties over with the pancake lifter to cook the other side. Cook for 2 minutes until golden brown and crispy.

3. Spread the mayonnaise on the bottom of each bun. Place 1 patty on top of mayonnaise. Top with lettuce. Cover with the top halves of the buns. Makes 4 buns.

Pictured on page 90.

- non-stick frying pan
- table knife
- pancake lifter
- bread knife
- cutting board

Hawaiian Grilled Cheese

The next best thing to visiting Hawaii.

1.			
Thin process cheese slices	2	2
Tub margarine, for spreading		
White (or whole wheat) bread slices	2	2
Tub margarine, for spreading		
Ham slice (1 oz., 28 g)	1	1
Pineapple slices, blotted very dry with paper towel	1-2	1-2

1. Heat the frying pan over medium-low heat. Spread the margarine on 1 side of each bread slice. Place 1 slice of cheese on the unbuttered side of each slice. Place the ham, pineapple and remaining slice of cheese over top. Lay the second slice of bread, buttered side up, on top of the cheese. Place the sandwich in the frying pan. When the bottom side is browned, flip the sandwich over to brown the other side. Cut in half on the cutting board. Makes 1 sandwich.

Pictured on page 36.

- non-stick frying pan
- table knife
- pancake lifter
- bread knife
- cutting board

Grilled Raisin & Cheese

Raisin bread adds lots of flavor to this classic!

1.			
Tub margarine, for spreading		
Raisin bread slices, buttered on one side	2	2
Process cheese slices (or your favorite cheese), to cover		

1. Heat the frying pan over medium-low heat. Spread the margarine on 1 side of each bread slice. Cover the unbuttered side of 1 slice of bread with the cheese. Lay the second slice of bread, buttered side up, on top of the cheese. Place the sandwich in the frying pan. When the bottom side is browned, flip the sandwich over to brown the other side. Cut in half on the cutting board. Makes 1 sandwich.

Egg Roll Buns hot

These take a little extra time, but they are worth it! Make these ahead and refrigerate or freeze. Reheat for your lunch.

1.			
Lean ground chicken	½ lb.	225 g	
Grated carrot	¼ cup	60 mL	
Finely chopped celery	¼ cup	60 mL	
Bean sprouts, chopped	½ cup	125 mL	
Chopped fresh mushrooms	¼ cup	60 mL	

2.			
Garlic powder	⅛ tsp.	0.5 mL	
Pepper, sprinkle			
Green onion, thinly sliced	1	1	
Black bean (or oyster) sauce	2 tbsp.	30 mL	

3.			
Refrigerator country-style biscuits (tube of 10)	12 oz.	340 g	

4.			
Large egg, fork-beaten	1	1	
Sesame seeds	1 tbsp.	15 mL	

- non-stick frying pan
- mixing spoon
- dry measures
- measuring spoons
- baking sheet
- table spoon
- pastry brush
- oven mitts
- wire rack

1. Scramble-fry the ground chicken in the frying pan over medium heat for 3 minutes. Add the carrot and celery. Scramble-fry for 3 to 5 minutes. Add the bean sprouts and mushrooms. Sauté until the liquid is gone.

2. Stir in the next 4 ingredients. Cook for about 2 minutes. Remove from the heat to cool. Makes 2 cups (500 mL).

3. Place the oven rack in the center position. Turn the oven on to 375°F (190°C). Grease the baking sheet. Open the biscuits and separate each and flatten into a 4 inch (10 cm) circle. Divide the filling evenly among the center of each circle. Bring the edges up and pinch together well to seal. Place seam side down on the baking sheet.

4. Using the pastry brush, brush the tops of each bun with the egg. Sprinkle with the sesame seeds. Bake in the oven for 15 to 16 minutes until golden. Use the oven mitts to remove the baking sheet to the wire rack. Makes 10 buns.

Pictured on page 17.

Sandwiches 117

Citrus Crunchies

Great to have on hand for the lunch bag or as a dessert snack.

1.	Tub margarine	2 tbsp.	30 mL
2.	Rice squares cereal	3 cups	750 mL
	Package lime, orange or grape-flavored gelatin (jelly powder), measure 3 tbsp., 50 mL	½ x **3 oz.**	½ x **85 g**

- measuring spoons
- microwave-safe cup
- microwave oven
- dry measures
- large bowl
- mixing spoon

1. Microwave the margarine in the cup on high (100%) for 20 to 30 seconds until melted.

2. Put the cereal into the bowl. Pour the melted margarine over the cereal. Toss until well coated. Sprinkle with the flavored gelatin. Toss together well. Microwave on high (100%) for 1 minute. Stir. Repeat 3 times. Makes 3 cups (750 mL).

Pictured on page 108.

Fruity Granola (hot)

Lots of nutty flavors. But sweetness comes through too.

1.	Large flake rolled oats (old-fashioned)	3 cups	750 mL
	Long thread coconut	½ cup	125 mL
	Slivered or sliced almonds	1 cup	250 mL
	Sesame seeds	2 tbsp.	30 mL
2.	Tub margarine	¼ cup	60 mL
	Liquid honey	3 tbsp.	50 mL
3.	Chopped dried fruit (such as cherries, apricots, raisins, apples or peaches)	2 cups	500 mL

- dry measures
- measuring spoons
- 2 large bowls
- mixing spoon
- liquid measures
- microwave oven
- baking sheet
- oven mitts
- wire rack

Continued on the next page.

1. Place the oven rack in the center position. Turn the oven on to 300°F (150°C). Combine the first 4 ingredients in the bowl. Stir.

2. Microwave the margarine and honey in the liquid measure on high (100%) for 1 minute until the margarine is melted and the mixture is bubbling. Pour over the rolled oat mixture and stir well to coat. Spread evenly on the ungreased baking sheet. Bake in the oven for 15 minutes. Stir well and spread the mixture out evenly once more. Bake for 10 minutes until golden brown. Use the oven mitts to remove the baking sheet to the wire rack. Cool.

3. Put the cooled mixture into the other bowl. Stir in the fruit. Makes 7 cups (1.75 L).

Pictured on page 107.

Toasted Pumpkin Seeds (hot)

What a treat around Halloween time! Just wash the fresh seeds well and dry them thoroughly on paper towels.

1.	**Tub margarine**	**1 tbsp.**	**15 mL**
2.	**Seasoning salt**	**½ tsp.**	**2 mL**
	Paprika	**¼ tsp.**	**1 mL**
	Hot pepper sauce, dash		
3.	**Hulled pumpkin seeds (fresh or from the bulk foods or health food store)**	**2 cups**	**500 mL**

- measuring spoons
- microwave-safe cup
- microwave oven
- mixing spoons
- dry measures
- medium bowl
- baking sheet
- oven mitts
- wire rack

1. Place the oven rack in the center position. Turn the oven on to 250°F (120°C). Microwave the margarine in the cup on high (100%) for 20 to 30 seconds until melted.

2. Stir in the next 3 ingredients.

3. Pour the mixture over the pumpkin seeds in the bowl. Toss well, using 2 spoons, to coat. Spread out on the ungreased baking sheet. Bake in the oven for 10 minutes. Stir. Bake in the oven for 10 minutes until crisp. Use the oven mitts to remove the baking sheet to the wire rack. Cool. Makes 2 cups (500 mL).

Pictured on page 108.

Bolts 'N' Things (hot)

Lots of different shapes—and flavors—in this. A bit spicy, a bit salty.

- dry measures
- small saucepan
- measuring spoons
- mixing spoon
- hot pad
- large bowl
- baking sheet
- oven mitts
- wire rack
- covered container

1.			
	Tub margarine	¼ cup	60 mL
	Worcestershire sauce	1 tbsp.	15 mL
	Seasoning salt	1 tsp.	5 mL
	Garlic powder	⅛ tsp.	0.5 mL
	Onion powder	⅛ tsp.	0.5 mL
2.			
	O-shaped toasted oat cereal	2 cups	500 mL
	Rice squares cereal	2 cups	500 mL
	Mini pretzels	2 cups	500 mL
	Cheese squares crackers	2 cups	500 mL
	Peanuts	1 cup	250 mL

1. Place the oven rack in the center position. Turn the oven on to 300°F (150°C). Melt the butter in the saucepan over medium heat. Stir in the next 4 ingredients. Remove the saucepan to the hot pad.

2. Combine the next 5 ingredients in the bowl. Slowly drizzle the butter mixture over the cereal mixture as you keep mixing. Spread on the ungreased baking sheet. Bake in the oven for 15 minutes. Stir well. Bake in the oven for 5 minutes until toasty looking. Use the oven mitts to remove the baking sheet to the wire rack. Cool. Store in the container. You may also freeze this. Makes 9 cups (2.25 L).

Use plastic containers to pack fragile cookies or muffins in your lunch bag. Plastic containers also work best for pickles, dip, salad dressing and other leaky lunch items. For added leakage protection, place a double layer of plastic wrap over the filled container and then put the lid on.

Peanut Butter Popcorn Treats (hot)

Just a hint of peanut butter and sweetness.

1.	Tub margarine	¼ cup	60 mL
2.	Brown sugar, packed	½ cup	125 mL
	Corn syrup	⅔ cup	150 mL
3.	Smooth peanut butter	½ cup	125 mL
	Vanilla flavoring	1 tsp.	5 mL
4.	Popped popcorn	8 cups	2 L

- dry measures
- small saucepan
- liquid measures
- mixing spoon
- hot pad
- measuring spoons
- large bowl
- baking sheet
- oven mitts
- wire rack
- covered container

1. Place the oven rack in the center position. Turn the oven on to 350°F (175°C). Melt the margarine in the saucepan over medium heat.

2. Stir in the sugar and corn syrup. Continue cooking until the sugar is dissolved.

3. Stir in the peanut butter. Bring the mixture to a boil. Remove from the heat to the hot pad. Stir in the vanilla flavoring.

4. Put the popcorn into the bowl. Pour the margarine mixture over the popcorn. Toss well to coat. Spread evenly on the ungreased baking sheet. Bake in the oven for 7 minutes. Use the oven mitts to remove the baking sheet to the wire rack. Cool. Break up the cooled popcorn into bite-size chunks. Store in the container. Makes 8 cups (2 L).

Pictured on page 89.

CHOCO-PEANUT BUTTER POPCORN BALLS: Add 2 tbsp. (30 mL) of cocoa along with the peanut butter to the dissolved sugar mixture in the saucepan. Bring to a boil. Remove from the heat. Add the vanilla flavoring. Pour over the popcorn. Toss well to coat. Cool popcorn mixture long enough so that you can handle it. Grease your hands and make tennis-size balls. Place on waxed paper to let them set. Makes about 14 balls.

Spicy Corn Corn

Unpopped popcorn will produce larger popped kernels when stored in an airtight container in the refrigerator or freezer.

- dry measures
- small saucepan
- measuring spoons
- mixing spoon
- hot pad
- large paper bag
- covered container

1.	Tub margarine	⅓ cup	75 mL
	Paprika	1 tsp.	5 mL
	Seasoning salt	½ tsp.	2 mL
	Chili powder	½ tsp.	2 mL
	Cayenne pepper	⅛ tsp.	0.5 mL
	Liquid smoke flavoring (optional)	1/16 tsp.	0.5 mL
2.	Warm popped popcorn (see Note)	8 cups	2 L
	Corn chips	2 cups	500 mL
	Peanuts (or mixed nuts)	1 cup	250 mL
	Grated Parmesan cheese (or Cheddar cheese powder)	3 tbsp.	50 mL

1. Melt the margarine in the saucepan over medium heat. Add the next 5 ingredients. Stir to combine. Remove the saucepan to the hot pad.

2. Combine the popped popcorn with the corn chips and peanuts in the paper bag. Stir the margarine mixture. Drizzle ⅓ over the popcorn mixture in the bag and add 1 tbsp. (15 mL) of the cheese. Shake the bag well to distribute the margarine and cheese. Repeat 2 times until all of the margarine and cheese are used up. Store any remaining popcorn in the container. Makes 10 cups (2.5 L).

Note: ¼ cup (60 mL) of unpopped popcorn kernels will make 8 cups of popped corn when made in a hot-air popcorn maker.

Easy Macaroni Soup

Chock full of pasta. Pale orange with bits of green and yellow from the vegetables. This can be warmed up the next day as a creamy mac 'n' cheese (as it will thicken overnight).

1.	**Water**	**4 cups**	**1 L**
	Seasoning salt	**½ tsp.**	**2 mL**
	Package of macaroni and cheese dinner, cheese flavor packet reserved	**6½ oz.**	**200 g**
2.	**Frozen mixed vegetables**	**1 cup**	**250 mL**
	Condensed chicken broth	**10 oz.**	**284 mL**
	Onion powder	**1 tsp.**	**5 mL**
	Pepper, sprinkle		
3.	**All-purpose flour**	**2 tbsp.**	**30 mL**
	Milk	**1 cup**	**250 mL**
	Reserved cheese flavor packet		

- liquid measures
- measuring spoons
- large saucepan
- mixing spoon
- dry measures
- small bowl
- whisk

1. Bring the water and seasoning salt to a boil in the saucepan. Add the macaroni only from the package. Boil for 5 minutes, stirring occasionally.

2. Add the vegetables, chicken broth, onion powder and pepper. Return to a boil and cook for 5 minutes.

3. Combine the flour and cheese flavor packet in the bowl. Slowly add the milk, whisking it until smooth. Add to the macaroni and vegetables in the saucepan. Cook, stirring constantly, for 2 or 3 minutes. Makes 7 cups (1.75 L).

Pictured on page 17.

- medium saucepan
- mixing spoon
- dry measures
- liquid measures
- measuring spoons

Hamburger Soup

Double the ingredients and make it for your family. Wholesome and hearty!

1.	Lean ground beef	½ lb.	225 g
2.	Finely chopped onion	¼ cup	60 mL
	Finely chopped celery	¼ cup	60 mL
3.	Medium carrot, cut in half lengthwise, then thinly sliced	1	1
	Medium potato, peeled and diced	1	1
	Water	3 cups	750 mL
	Beef bouillon powder	1 tbsp.	15 mL
4.	Condensed tomato soup	10 oz.	284 mL

1. Scramble-fry the ground beef in the saucepan until no longer pink. Drain off fat.

2. Stir in the onion and celery. Scramble-fry for 3 minutes.

3. Stir in the carrot, potato, water and bouillon powder. Bring to a boil over medium-high heat. Reduce the heat to medium-low. Partially cover, moving the lid slightly to the side to allow a small opening for the steam to escape. Simmer for 20 minutes.

4. Stir in the tomato soup. Heat thoroughly. Makes 5 cups (1.25 L).

Pictured on the back cover.

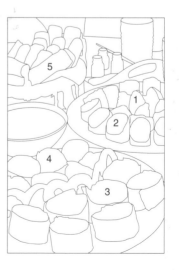

1. Smoked Salmon Spread, page 33
2. Jam & Cheese Spread, page 37
3. "Wurst" Cheese & Lettuce Wrap, page 135
4. Roast Beef Rolls, page 132
5. Pizza Sticks (with Dipping Sauce), page 84

Vegetable Chowder

Break up the noodles before you open the package—it's a lot less messy.

1.	Tub margarine	1 tbsp.	15 mL
	Small onion, chopped	1	1
	Celery rib, chopped	1	1
	Grated carrot	¼ cup	60 mL
2.	Large potato, with peel, diced	1	1
	Water	5 cups	1.25 L
	Vegetable (or chicken) bouillon powder	1 tbsp.	15 mL
3.	Package instant noodle soup with flavor packet	3 oz.	100 g

- measuring spoons
- large saucepan
- dry measures
- mixing spoon
- liquid measures

1. Melt the margarine in the saucepan over medium heat. Add the onion, celery and carrot. Sauté until the onion is soft.

2. Stir in the potato, water and bouillon powder. Partially cover, moving the lid slightly to the side to allow a small opening for the steam to escape. Simmer for 15 minutes.

3. Break up the noodles and add, along with the flavor packet, to the simmering mixture in the saucepan. Simmer for 10 minutes. Makes 7 cups (1.75 L).

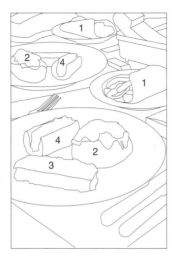

1. Mexican Stir-Fry Sandwich, page 131
2. Mushroom Swiss Potato, page 76
3. Quick Turkey Loaf, page 56
4. Rice Salad, page 92

Corn Chowder

Crunchy veggies and thicker creamy base. So quick to make on a cold day.

1.	**Bacon slices, diced**	**2**	**2**
2.	**Chopped onion**	**¼ cup**	**60 mL**
	Chopped green or red pepper	**¼ cup**	**60 mL**
	All-purpose flour	**1 tbsp.**	**15 mL**
	Milk	**1 cup**	**250 mL**
	Canned cream-style corn	**14 oz.**	**398 mL**
3.	**Parsley flakes**	**1 tsp.**	**5 mL**
	Hot pepper sauce, dash		
	Pepper, sprinkle		

- medium saucepan
- mixing spoon
- dry measures
- measuring spoons
- liquid measures
- hot pad

1. Fry the bacon in the saucepan over medium heat until crisp. Drain off fat.

2. Add the onion and pepper. Cook for 2 minutes until soft. Sprinkle the flour over the vegetables. Stir together well. Slowly stir in the milk and corn. Bring just to a simmer. Remove the saucepan to the hot pad.

3. Add the remaining 3 ingredients. Stir. Makes 3 cups (750 mL).

Pictured on page 72.

To keep soups nice and warm until lunch, preheat your thermos at the last possible moment before filling it. First, fill the thermos with boiling water and let stand for 5 minutes. Pour out the hot water. Fill the thermos with the hot soup. Seal it tightly.

Bean 'N' Bacon Soup

Make this as zippy as you want with the hot pepper sauce. This is a chunky soup with lots of liquid.

1.	Bacon slices, diced	2	2
	Small onion, chopped	1	1
2.	Large potato, peeled and diced	1	1
	Water	2 cups	500 mL
3.	Condensed vegetable soup	10 oz.	284 mL
	Canned beans in tomato sauce, mashed with a fork	14 oz.	398 mL
	Hot pepper sauce	$^{1}/_{8}$-$^{1}/_{4}$ tsp.	0.5-1 mL
4.	Grated Cheddar cheese, sprinkle (for garnish)		

- large saucepan
- mixing spoon
- liquid measures
- measuring spoons

1. Fry the bacon in the saucepan over medium heat for 2 minutes. Add the onion. Sauté for about 5 minutes until the bacon is cooked and the onion is soft.

2. Add the potato and water. Cover and bring to a boil over medium heat for 10 to 12 minutes until the potato is tender.

3. Stir in the vegetable soup, beans and pepper sauce. Simmer, uncovered, for 10 minutes.

4. Garnish with Cheddar cheese. Makes 5$^{1}/_{2}$ cups (1.3 L).

Pictured on page 71.

Variation: Substitute condensed cream of celery soup or condensed cream of mushroom soup for the vegetable soup.

- measuring spoons
- large saucepan
- dry measures
- mixing spoon
- liquid measures

Color-Full Bean Soup

Tasty balance of flavors between the ham and the beans. Name says it all.

1.	Tub margarine	1 tbsp.	15 mL
	Chopped onion	½ cup	125 mL
	Chopped celery	½ cup	125 mL
2.	Medium carrot, grated	1	1
	Water	2 cups	500 mL
	Medium potato, peeled and diced	1	1
	Canned mixed beans, with liquid	19 oz.	540 mL
	Bay leaf	1	1
	Chili powder	½ tsp.	2 mL
	Parsley flakes	½ tsp.	2 mL
	Pepper	⅛ tsp.	0.5 mL
3.	Canned flakes of ham, crumbled (or ½ cup, 125 mL, finely chopped cooked ham)	6.5 oz.	184 g

1. Melt the margarine in the saucepan over medium heat. Sauté the onion and celery until soft.

2. Add the next 8 ingredients. Bring to a boil. Reduce the heat to low. Cover. Simmer for 20 minutes.

3. Add the ham. Stir. Cover and simmer for 5 minutes. Makes 6 cups (1.5 L).

Did you know?

Whenever you're cooking something on the stove, it's wise to fit your pan size to the burner size—don't put a small pan on a great big burner! For safety, turn pan handles so they don't stick out over the edge of the stove, but make sure they're not over another burner.

Mexican Stir-Fry Sandwich

Lots of color! Great taste! Change the spiciness according to your preference.

1.	**Cooking oil**	**1 tsp.**	**5 mL**
	Boneless, skinless chicken breast half (about 4 oz., 113 g), slivered	**1**	**1**
2.	**Garlic powder**	**¹⁄₈ tsp.**	**0.5 mL**
	Salt	**¹⁄₈ tsp.**	**0.5 mL**
	Pepper	**¹⁄₁₆ tsp.**	**0.5 mL**
3.	**Small red (or other mild) onion, thinly sliced**	**¹⁄₂**	**¹⁄₂**
	Medium green, red or yellow pepper, slivered	**¹⁄₂**	**¹⁄₂**
	Salsa	**¹⁄₃ cup**	**75 mL**
4.	**White (or whole wheat) flour tortillas (8-10 inch, 20-25 cm, size)**	**3**	**3**

- measuring spoons
- frying pan
- mixing spoon
- dry measures
- hot pad

1. Heat the cooking oil in the frying pan over medium-high heat. Stir-fry the chicken for 2 minutes.

2. Add the garlic powder, salt and pepper. Cook for 2 minutes.

3. Add the onion and green pepper to the chicken. Stir-fry for 3 minutes. Add the salsa and stir-fry for 2 minutes until the vegetables are tender-crisp. Remove the frying pan to the hot pad. Makes 2 cups (500 mL).

4. Divide the mixture evenly among the 3 tortillas. Fold, envelope-style, by bringing the bottom edge of the tortilla to the center, over the chicken mixture. Fold the left side over the center and then fold the right side over the center, overlapping the left side. Makes 3 smaller tortilla sandwiches.

Pictured on page 126.

Pictured on page 126.

Wraps & Rolls

Roast Beef Rolls chill

Try these dipped in Honey Mustard Dunk, page 28.

- measuring spoons
- table knife
- dry measures
- plastic wrap

1.			
Plain (or herbed) spreadable cream cheese	3 tbsp.	50 mL
White (or whole wheat) flour tortilla (10 inch, 25 cm, size)	1	1
Shredded lettuce	½ cup	125 mL
Finely diced onion	1 tbsp.	15 mL
Shaved roast beef (or 3 very thin slices)	2 oz.	56 g

1. Spread the cream cheese on 1 side of the tortilla. Cover with the lettuce and onion. Lay the beef over top. Roll up tightly and wrap with plastic wrap. Chill in the refrigerator for at least 1 hour or overnight. Makes 1 roll.

Pictured on page 125.

Lettuce Rolls chill

These are best made in the morning before school. Lettuce leaves will become soggy if rolls are made the night before. Peel down the plastic wrap as you eat the roll.

- measuring spoons
- table knife
- plastic wrap

1.			
Large lettuce leaves	4	4
Ham slices (or other sliced deli meat)	2	2
Prepared mustard (or mayonnaise)	1 tbsp.	15 mL

1. Lay lettuce leaves on the working surface, making 2 stacks of 2 lettuce leaves each. Lay 1 slice of ham over each lettuce stack. Spread mustard over the ham. Roll up tightly and wrap with plastic wrap. Chill in the refrigerator. Makes 2 rolls.

Variation: Place a carrot stick, cheese stick, dill pickle wedge or folded cheese slice on the top of the ham before rolling.

Ham & Cheese Delights (hot)

Take one or two of these for your school lunch. Great warm or cold.

1.	Cream cheese, softened	8 oz.	250 g
	Sweet pickle relish	1½ tbsp.	25 mL
	Ham slices, diced	5	5
	Onion powder	¼ tsp.	1 mL
2.	Refrigerator crescent-style rolls (tube of 8)	8 oz.	235 g

- measuring spoons
- medium bowl
- mixing spoon
- table knife
- baking sheet
- oven mitts
- wire rack

1. Place the oven rack in the center position. Turn the oven on to 375°F (190°C). Combine the cream cheese, relish, ham and onion powder in the bowl. Mix well.

2. Open the crescent roll tube and separate the rolls into 8 triangles. Spread 2 tbsp. (30 mL) of the ham mixture on each triangle. Roll from the shortest side of the triangle to the opposite point. Place the rolls on the ungreased baking sheet. Bake in the oven for 12 minutes until golden brown. Use the oven mitts to remove the baking sheet to the wire rack. Makes 8 "delights."

Pictured on page 107.

Did you know?

Flour tortillas keep well in a sealed plastic bag in the refrigerator for up to 2 weeks. They can even be frozen. Be creative and use flour tortillas the next time you reach for the bread slices.

Corn Doggies hot

Make these the night before and simply reheat for lunch. These also freeze well.

- medium bowl
- dry measures
- measuring spoons
- table fork
- rolling pin
- ruler
- table knife
- pastry brush
- baking sheet
- oven mitts
- wire rack

1.			
Envelope pie crust mix	1 x 9½ oz.	1 x 270 g
Cornmeal	⅓ cup	75 mL
Chili powder	1 tsp.	5 mL
Cold water, approximately	6 tbsp.	100 mL
All-purpose flour, as needed, to prevent sticking when rolling		

2.			
Wieners	8	8
Large egg, fork-beaten	1	1

1. Place the oven rack in the center position. Turn the oven on to 450°F (230°F). Pour the pie crust mix into the bowl. Stir in the cornmeal and chili powder. Slowly add the cold water, 1 tbsp. (15 mL) at a time, stirring with a fork after each addition. The dough should start to pull away from the sides of the bowl and form a ball. Divide in half. Roll each half into a 5 x 12 inch (12.5 x 30 cm) rectangle on a lightly floured counter or working surface. Cut each rectangle crosswise into 4 equal rectangles.

2. Place a wiener lengthwise across each rectangle. Brush 1 of the long edges of the pastry with the egg. Bring the 2 long edges of the rectangle up over the wiener and press together to seal. Place seam side down on the ungreased baking sheet. Repeat with each rectangle. Brush each surface with remaining egg. Bake in the oven for 12 minutes until crisp and golden. Use the oven mitts to remove the baking sheet to the wire rack. Makes 8 wrapped wieners.

Pictured on page 71.

"Wurst" Cheese & Lettuce Wrap chill

Very easy and quick to make. Spread as much liverwurst on the tortilla as you like.

1.
Plain (or herbed) liverwurst	2-3 tbsp.	30-50 mL
White (or whole wheat) flour tortilla (10 inch, 25 cm, size)	1	1
Grated Swiss cheese	⅓ cup	75 mL
Shredded lettuce	⅓-½ cup	75-125 mL

- measuring spoons
- table knife
- dry measures
- plastic wrap

1. Spread the liverwurst on the tortilla. Sprinkle with the cheese and lettuce. Roll up tightly and wrap with plastic wrap. Chill in the refrigerator. Makes 1 wrap.

Pictured on page 125.

Vegetable Roll chill

Try different flavored dressings for a variety of tastes.

1.
Spreadable cream cheese	1 tbsp.	15 mL
Ranch (or other creamy) dressing	1 tbsp.	15 mL
White (or whole wheat) flour tortilla (10 inch, 25 cm, size)	1	1

2.
Grated carrot	2 tbsp.	30 mL
Finely chopped green, red or yellow pepper	2 tbsp.	30 mL
Finely chopped green onion	2 tsp.	10 mL
Finely chopped broccoli florets	3 tbsp.	50 mL
Grated Cheddar cheese	¼ cup	60 mL

- measuring spoons
- small bowl
- mixing spoon
- table knife
- dry measures
- plastic wrap

1. Combine the cream cheese and dressing in the bowl. Stir. Spread the cream cheese mixture on the tortilla, almost to the edge.

2. Sprinkle with the remaining 5 ingredients in the order given. Roll up tightly and wrap with plastic wrap. Chill in the refrigerator. Makes 1 roll.

Pictured on page 18.

Cucumber Under Wraps  chill

Pack these for your lunch. Easy to eat.

- measuring spoons
- table knife
- plastic wrap

1.	Plain (or herbed) spreadable cream cheese	½ cup	125 mL
	White (or whole wheat) flour tortillas (8 inch, 20 cm, size)	4	4
2.	English cucumber piece, 6 inches (15 cm) long, quartered lengthwise	1	1
	Salt, sprinkle (optional)		
	Pepper, sprinkle (optional)		

1. Spread 2 tbsp. (30 mL) of the cream cheese on each tortilla.

2. Lay 1 cucumber spear across 1 side of each tortilla. Sprinkle with salt and pepper. Roll each tortilla around the cucumber. Wrap tightly with plastic wrap. Chill in the refrigerator. Makes 4 rolls.

Peanut Butter Wrap chill

Much more fun than your ordinary peanut butter sandwich.

- measuring spoons
- table knife
- dry measures
- small cup
- small spoon
- plastic wrap

1.	Peanut butter	2 tbsp.	30 mL
	White (or whole wheat) flour tortilla (10 inch, 25 cm, size)	1	1
	Chopped apple, with peel	½ cup	125 mL
2.	Brown sugar, packed	1 tsp.	5 mL
	Ground cinnamon	¼ tsp.	1 mL

1. Spread the peanut butter on the tortilla. Scatter the apple over the top.

2. Combine the sugar and cinnamon in the cup. Sprinkle over the apple. Roll tortilla up tightly and wrap with plastic wrap. Chill in the refrigerator. Makes 1 roll.

Wraps & Rolls

measurement tables

hroughout this book measurements are given in Conventional and Metric measures. The tables below provide a quick reference for the standard measures, weights, temperatures, and sizes.

Spoons

Conventional Measure	Metric Standard Measure Millilitre (mL)
1/8 teaspoon (tsp.)	0.5 mL
1/4 teaspoon (tsp.)	1 mL
1/2 teaspoon (tsp.)	2 mL
1 teaspoon (tsp.)	5 mL
2 teaspoons (tsp.)	10 mL
1 tablespoon (tbsp.)	15 mL

Cups

Conventional Measure	Metric Standard Measure Millilitre (mL)
1/4 cup (4 tbsp.)	60 mL
1/3 cup (5 1/3 tbsp.)	75 mL
1/2 cup (8 tbsp.)	125 mL
2/3 cup (10 2/3 tbsp.)	150 mL
3/4 cup (12 tbsp.)	175 mL
1 cup (16 tbsp.)	250 mL
4 cups	1000 mL (1 L)

Weights

Ounces (oz.)	Grams (g)
1 oz.	30 g
2 oz.	55 g
3 oz.	85 g
4 oz.	125 g
5 oz.	140 g
6 oz.	170 g
7 oz.	200 g
8 oz.	250 g
16 oz. (1 lb.)	454 g
32 oz. (2 lbs.)	900 g
35 oz. (2.2 lbs.)	1000 g (1 kg)

Oven Temperatures

Fahrenheit (°F)	Celsius (°C)
175°	80°
200°	95°
225°	110°
250°	120°
275°	140°
300°	150°
325°	160°
350°	175°
375°	190°
400°	205°
425°	220°
450°	230°
475°	240°
500°	260°

Pans

Conventional Inches	Metric Centimetres
8x8 inch	20x20 cm
9x9 inch	22x22 cm
9x13 inch	22x33 cm
10x15 inch	25x38 cm
11x17 inch	28x43 cm
8x2 inch round	20x5 cm
9x2 inch round	22x5 cm
10x4 1/2 inch tube	25x11 cm
8x4x3 inch loaf	20x10x7.5 cm
9x5x3 inch loaf	22x12.5x7.5 cm

Casseroles

Conventional Quart (qt.)	Metric Litre (L)
1 qt.	1 L
1 1/2 qt.	1.5 L
2 qt.	2 L
2 1/2 qt.	2.5 L
3 qt.	3 L
4 qt.	4 L

index

139

Mail Order Form

Company's Coming cookbooks are available at retail locations everywhere!

Buy 2 Get 1 FREE!
Buy 2 cookbooks—get 1 of equal value **ABSOLUTELY FREE!**

$19.99 ASSORTED TITLES
Also available in French

INDICATE QUANTITY		
BUY	**FREE**	
		Company's Coming for Christmas* (hardcover)
		Easy Entertaining* (hardcover) ◄NEW► Oct 98
		Beef Today! (softcover)

No. of Books Purchased (Do not include FREE books)

[   ] X [$19.99] = [$]

Choose 1 FREE book for every 2 books of equal value purchased

---

$14.99 ASSORTED TITLES
Also available in French

INDICATE QUANTITY				INDICATE QUANTITY		
BUY	**FREE**			**BUY**	**FREE**	
		The Family Table				Kids - Snacks*
		Low-fat Cooking*				Company's Coming for Kids - Lunches ◄NEW► July 98

No. of Books Purchased (Do not include FREE books)

[   ] X [$14.99] = [$]

Choose 1 FREE book for every 2 books of equal value purchased

---

$12.99 COMPANY'S COMING SERIES
Also available in French

INDICATE QTY BUY	FREE		INDICATE QTY BUY	FREE		INDICATE QTY BUY	FREE		INDICATE QTY BUY	FREE	
		150 Delicious Squares*			Cookies*			Lunches*			Kids Cooking*
		Casseroles*			Vegetables			Pies*			Fish & Seafood*
		Muffins & More*			Main Courses			Light Recipes*			Breads*
		Salads*			Pasta*			Microwave Cooking*			Meatless Cooking*
		Appetizers			Cakes			Preserves*			Cooking For Two*
		Desserts			Barbecues*			Light Casseroles*			Breakfasts & Brunches*
		Soups & Sandwiches			Dinners of the World			Chicken, Etc.*			Slow Cooker Recipes ◄NEW► Sept 98
		Holiday Entertaining*									

No. of Books Purchased (Do not include FREE books)

[   ] X [$12.99] = [$]

Choose 1 FREE book for every 2 books of equal value purchased

---

$9.99 SELECT SERIES
Also available in French

INDICATE QUANTITY				INDICATE QUANTITY		
BUY	**FREE**			**BUY**	**FREE**	
		Sauces & Marinades*				30-Minute Meals*
		Ground Beef*				Make-Ahead Salads*
		Beans & Rice*				No-Bake Desserts*

No. of Books Purchased (Do not include FREE books)

[   ] X [$9.99] = [$]

Choose 1 FREE book for every 2 books of equal value purchased

---

Make cheque or money order payable to: **COMPANY'S COMING PUBLISHING LIMITED**
- **ORDERS OUTSIDE OF CANADA:** Must be paid in U.S. funds by cheque or money order drawn on Canadian or U.S. bank, or by credit card.
- Rush courier rates available on request. Please call our Shipping Department (403) 450-6223 for details.
- Prices subject to change without prior notice.
- Sorry, no C.O.D.'s.
- Bill my MasterCard or Visa (please check one) ○ MasterCard ○ VISA _____

Expiry Date _____

Account # _____

Name of Cardholder _____

Cardholder's Signature _____

TOTAL PRICE FOR ALL BOOKS	$
Plus Shipping & Handling (for each destination)	$ 5.00
SUB-TOTAL	$
Canadian residents add G.S.T. / H.S.T. (7%)	$
TOTAL AMOUNT ENCLOSED	$

One low rate for shipping & handling—ANY SIZE ORDER!!

○ **YES! Please send a catalogue.** ○ **English** ○ **French**

gift giving

DID YOU KNOW that we also have other books just for kids? Be sure to check out *Kids Cooking* from our Company's Coming softcover series, and our colorful cookbook *Snacks,* for great recipes you can make on your own. We also have other books that would make great gifts for your friends and family—just fill out the form below with the names and addresses of the people you'd like to send them to, and we'll deliver the books right to their door. If you'd like to include your personal note or card, we'll be happy to enclose it with your gift order.

SHIPPING ADDRESS

Send the Company's Coming Cookbooks listed on the reverse side of this coupon, to:

Name: _____

Street: _____

City: _____

Province/State: _____

Postal Code/Zip: _____

Tel: ( ) _____

E-mail Address (if applicable): _____

Company's Coming cookbooks are available at retail locations everywhere.

For information contact:

Company's Coming
COOKBOOKS®

Company's Coming Publishing Limited
2311 - 96 Street Edmonton, Alberta, Canada T6N 1G3
Tel: (403) 450-6223   Fax: (403) 450-1857
e-mail: info@companyscoming.com • www.companyscoming.com